S0-BIY-970

STOLEN APPLES

Other titles by Yevgeny Yevtushenko published in this country:

SELECTED POEMS
trans. by R. Milner-Gulland and Peter Levi.

A PRECOCIOUS AUTOBIOGRAPHY

SELECTED POETRY
trans. R. Milner-Gulland.

POETRY
by Evtushenko, Pasternak, Akhmatove.

POEMS CHOSEN BY THE AUTHOR
trans. P. Levi and R. Milner-Gulland.

THE POETRY OF YEVGENY YEVTUSHENKO
1953-1965, trans. G. Reavey. *Bilingual text.*

THE BRATSK STATION AND OTHER POEMS
trans. T. T. Glassner and others.

YEVTUSHENKO POEMS
trans. H. Marshall. *Bilingual text.*

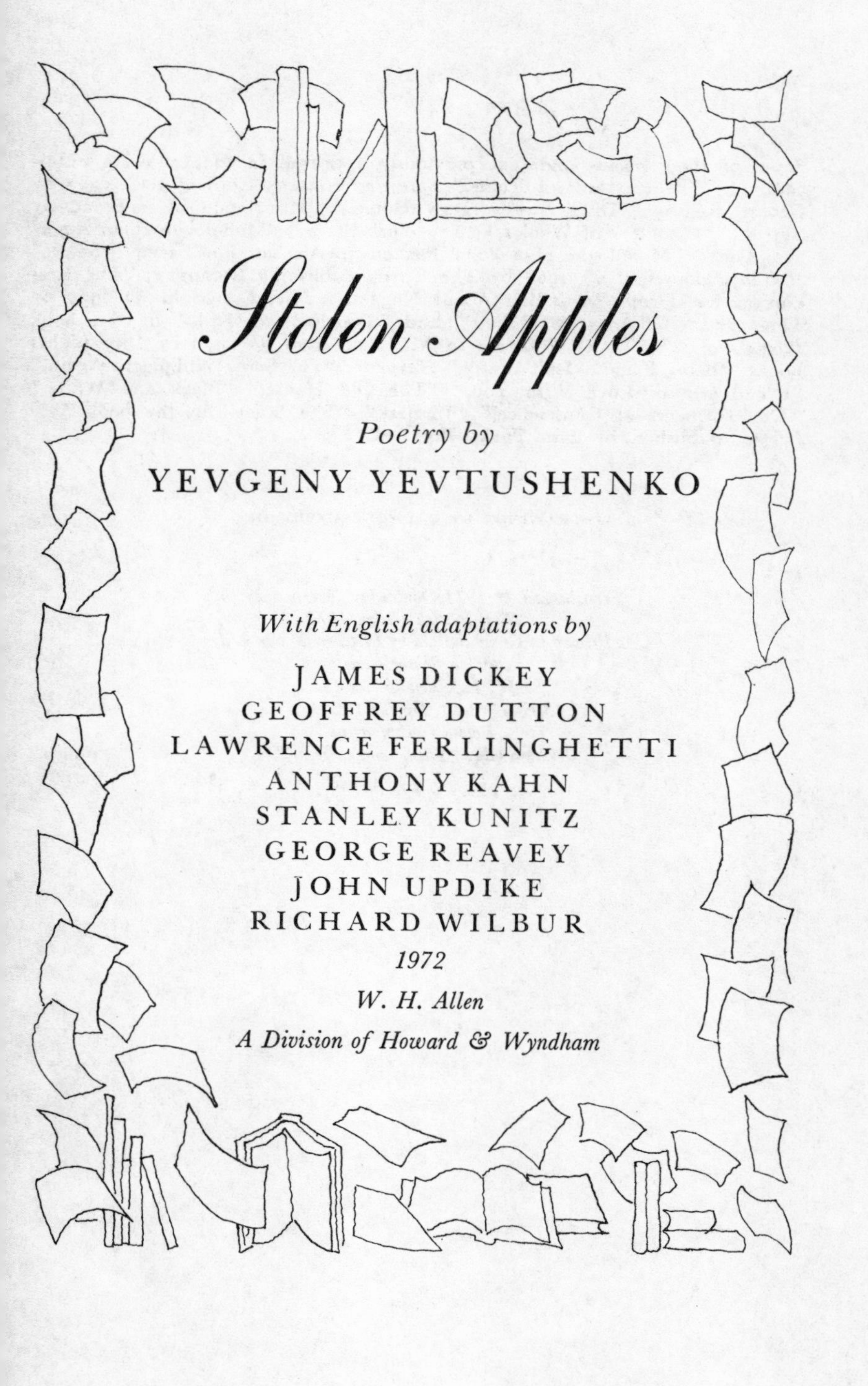

Stolen Apples

Poetry by

YEVGENY YEVTUSHENKO

With English adaptations by

JAMES DICKEY
GEOFFREY DUTTON
LAWRENCE FERLINGHETTI
ANTHONY KAHN
STANLEY KUNITZ
GEORGE REAVEY
JOHN UPDIKE
RICHARD WILBUR

1972

W. H. Allen
A Division of Howard & Wyndham

Some of these poems and text previously appeared in the following publications: "The Rhythms of Rome," *Saturday Review,* Copyright © 1967 by George Reavey; "In a Steelworker's Home," "Monologue of a Broadway Actress," "Cemetery of Whales," "New York Elegy," "Monologue of an American Poet," "Monologue of a Polar Fox on an Alaskan Fur Farm," "Smog," *Holiday,* Copyright © 1968 by The Curtis Publishing Company; "The Restaurant for Two," "A Ballad About Nuggets," *Life,* Copyright © 1967 by Time Inc.; "Flowers & Bullets" and "Freedom to Kill," in the book *Flowers and Bullets & Freedom to Kill,* Copyright © 1970 by City Lights Books; "Being Famous Isn't Pretty," *Harper's;* "The Snow Will Begin Again," "I Fell Out of Love With You," "The Old House," "Black and White," "The Torments of Conscience," "In Jest," "The Stage" in the book *New Poems,* published by Sun Books Pty Ltd.

DRAWINGS BY RAYMOND DAVIDSON

First British edition 1972
Printed in Great Britain by Fletcher & Son Ltd,
Norwich for the publishers
W. H. Allen & Co. Ltd,
43 Essex Street, London WC2R 3JG
Bound in Bungay by
Richard Clay (The Chaucer Press) Ltd.

ISBN 0 491 00199 1

Poetry gives off smoke
but it doesn't die out.
It acts kind of crazy, flutteringly,
when it chooses us.

CONTENTS

I. КАЧКА

II. ТВИСТ НА ГВОЗДЯХ

CONTENTS

III. THE TORMENTS OF CONSCIENCE

V. PROCESSION WITH THE MADONNA

V. КЛАДБИЩЕ КИТОВ

V. CEMETERY OF WHALES

BEING FAMOUS ISN'T PRETTY

In taking this line from Pasternak as the title for my foreword, I've acted without arrogance or self-disparagement, a thing far worse than pride. Let me assure my readers of that. Not that in my poetic adolescence I didn't dream of fame. I did. Nor will I say that now when I write poetry or even this foreword I'm indifferent to the opinion of my readers. That would also be a lie. But fame is a far from charming mistress. She demands endless gifts and tokens of affection; she gets hysterical, jealous; she makes me quarrel with my friends, kills my concentration, drags me off on senseless visits, threatens me with abandonment. Many envy me such a spectacular prize. If they lived with her a while they'd change their minds. But then, jealousy never admits to being itself. It hides behind its own suspicions: "What crooked route led that fellow to glory? After all, we're honest and yet, unknown."

And so, legends of suspicion arise with the myths of praise. And when you've heard enough of them about yourself, you're bound to lose your bearings and wonder fearfully who you really are. If you live under the magnifying glass of public curiosity, just as your every honest act seems heroic to some, so your every weakness seems criminal to others. Even your honest acts come into question. Of course, where there's smoke there's fire, but the smoke of a myth can sometimes obscure the nature of the fire. Fame is the Medusa's head, horrid and hissing with the snakes of gossip. To look in her face is to turn to stone, even if they call the stone a monument. You need the trusty shield of Perseus to see a safe reflection of your fame. At the start of his journey an artist must struggle for fame; once it's been won, he must learn how to struggle with it.

When I read certain articles about myself in the West I wonder who in the hell this damned "Y.Y." can be. A movie star, tanned by photographers' flashbulbs? A matador, teasing his red cape in the bull's snout of the age? A tightrope walker, toeing the slack wire between East and West? Or, as one of England's ex-angry-young-men Kingsley Amis hinted, an unofficial diplomat, performing certain secret missions for the Kremlin? A rebellious Stenka Razin,* as a laureate of the Goncourt Prize, Armand Lanoux, once wrote? Or maybe a nice, inquisitive traveler, as the magazine *America,* distributed in the USSR, once had it, asking everyone to call him "just Zhenya." A Soviet Beatle? An export item, perhaps, like vodka or black caviar? A conformist masquerading as a champion of liberalization? A radical in moderate's clothing? Or are all these mere ingredients blended in the shaker of the age into a strange cocktail called Yevtushenko?

On the one hand, he's in the fight against anti-Semitism, bureaucratism, etc. You'd like to take the lanky Russian in your arms and whisper to him confidentially, "We're with you in your selfless struggle." On the other hand, he doesn't much care for Western society. In fact, he harshly indicts it for the war in Vietnam, the murders of Martin Luther King and the Kennedys, for bigotry, hypocrisy, and corruption. You get suspicious: If this Russian is really on the side of truth, an honest man in a totalitarian society, what's he doing out of jail? Why does he go abroad from time to time, and then unaccompanied by commissars? Isn't he perhaps a commissar himself?

An aerial diver in a suit, his luggage bulging with hidden microfilms, even went so far as to say that, according to information at his disposal, one out of every two Soviet writers abroad was an agent of the Secret Police, that if one of them traveled alone he was an agent for sure, and that someday Yevtushenko would have to render

* Razin was a leader of a Cossack and peasant rebellion on Russia's southeastern frontier in the late 1660s. He was captured by Cossacks loyal to Moscow and, in 1671, tortured and executed in the capital. [A.K.]

an account of the reports he wrote on returning home. In his haste he apparently forgot that somewhat earlier in his fascinating confession he admitted informing on that same Yevtushenko as a leader of an intelligentsia underground center. Amazing, isn't it, this charming little contradiction?

But the most amazing thing of all happened in 1967 in Santiago de Chile. There, on the day of my reading, two groups of young people organized demonstrations against me on two different squares. On one, the solemn "ultra-leftists" burned me in effigy as an American spy. On the other the "ultra-rightists" burned me as a Red spy. To be honest, I was pleasantly surprised to find these charming youths rating my services as high as those of some latter-day Mata Hari.

When in 1968 English students supported me as a candidate for the position of Oxford's Professor of Poetry, God! how the aforementioned Amis & Company put me to the knife, calling me a wily propagandist, an official mouthpiece of the Soviet government, and on and on. Again, I was pleasantly surprised that my social standing in the USSR seemed so strong. And after all the noise about me as a political agent extraordinaire, there suddenly came the quiet voices of Arthur Miller and William Styron, both of them *obliged to announce that, in their opinion, I was an honest man.* And the voice of my translator, Robin Milner Holland, *compelled to explain that I was a poet,* and not something else.

Even in his own country people not too familiar with this strange fellow, this Yevtushenko, can be found. For the radicals I'm too moderate, for the liberals too radical, for perfervid dogmatists, almost the devil himself. In a lamentably much discussed novel, one writer, depicting a traitor to the Motherland, a fascist collaborator hiding from retribution, even went so far as to put some of my verses on his lips. One poet in his time accused me of being unpatriotic. "What kind of Russian are you," he said, "when you've forgotten your own people?" They've called me a "singer of dirty bedsheets," a "poet of the mod set," and more. To lovers of the philosophical lyric I seem too simplistic, to lovers of the intimate lyric, too rational—a pamphleteer. And to others who interpret poetry only politically, too ambivalent.

Lovers of political poetry, incidentally, are themselves rather sharply split in two. The first group applauds all my lines that condemn Western society and praise the Motherland. "There, that's the way he should always write." But let one line about our ills drop from my pen and they're at me: "There he is, messing around in the wrong country again." They're a suspicious group. Even in my poems about other countries they detect hints directed at our own, and in poems about the pre-Revolutionary past, dangerous allusions to the present.

The second group is the opposite of the first. They take offense at political poems dealing, say, with Vietnam, or the glories of the Motherland, seeing in them no sincere movement of the soul but a political maneuver to gain the favor of those in power. Just as the first group, deaf to their neighbor's groan behind the wall, listens only to the bombs in Vietnam, so the second thinks the problems of the world are nothing next to their aching corns. The second group wants only negative poems on domestic problems. Somehow they find it morally questionable to speak of the corruption of the Western world when in the Soviet Union the price of cognac is on the rise, the meat supply uncertain, and the stores, in general, unjust.

When, then, you ask, is Yevtushenko sincere? When writing of Vietnam or Babi Yar? There isn't much profit in defending yourself, but, alas, I must.

It's easy to forget the simple fact that a man can speak sincerely of both Vietnam and Babi Yar, and in both a major and a minor key. Art in general is higher than questions of "for" or "against" alone. Art is a rainbow broad enough even for black. But a rainbow stretched across two shores casts all its colors equally on each. It doesn't leave one side in bright light and the other in the dark.

Injustice is as widely traveled as justice, and a scoundrel with an American passport is no better than a louse with a Soviet one. As Mayakovsky once said, "The widest choice of scoundrels roams through our land and about."

I know, of course, that this one world is really two, even, as they say, three, and tomorrow, maybe four. Still, I think our old, good woman Earth, though torn by political conflict, is the only world we have and we're all her tenants depending in one way or another on each other. A little-known Russian poet, Stefanovich, put it this way:

All of us share one lot.
Just sprain your ankle
And instantly in Addis Ababa
Someone shrieks in pain.

And so, I write poems about Vietnam and Babi Yar and Kent University student Allison Krause and a Siberian concrete-pourer, Nyushka, and a general in the army of freedom, Pancho Villa, and my own mother, who lost her voice singing concerts in snowstorms on the front lines, and a Chilean prostitute who hung a portrait of Leo Tolstoy in her closet and Sicilian women in black and young girls in white and my own beloved and my son and myself. I want to be a mail boat for everyone divided by the ice of estrangement, a craft before the coming of large navigation, moving through the drifting ice with letters and parcels.

Still, sometimes I deeply resent being discussed as a political personality and not as a poet, and having my poetry examined on the whole from one political standpoint or another. Of course, Heinrich Boll was right when he said that everything published was already committed. Every writer is committed by his conscience and his talent, even if he declares himself "above the fray."

It's a disgrace to be free of your age.
A hundred times more shameful than to be its slave.

I don't want to be free from the struggle for freedom. But I do want to be free to determine the forms it will take. Although I once had the indiscretion to say that a poet in Russia is more than a poet, I've never pretended to be a political prophet. In politics I'm undoubtedly a dilettante, even though my loathing for professional politicking prompts me to think it will be a great day for mankind when its politics are in the hands of amateurs rather than professionals.

Compared to the refined, cold master Salieri, who "verified his harmonies with algebra," Mozart must have seemed a dilettante. But it was Mozart, and not Salieri, who advanced the development of the world's music. History flows to the laws of music, and the Mozarts of the world are her masters. Blok's rallying call "Listen to the music of the Revolution!" is eternal, for revolution is protean and, despite what pessimists may say, the revolution in human consciousness will never end.

You can wave art aside as a weapon in that revolution if you want; it's true, for all the beauty art creates, mankind wallows every day in the filth of its inhumanity. But I'm bold enough to believe that if there is anything exalted in man, if the revolution in consciousness still goes on, by that much is mankind indebted to art.

In the long run I don't much care who picks me to pieces or how, or who puts me in what category. I know that I'm one of the workmen of art, that I toil in her hot, unhealthy shop, poetry, and that this is the meaning of my life. Politically untutored and forever concerned with those little things that so enrich our suffering lives with beauty, I've never formulated any new political concepts. I've only reminded people of the commonplaces of good and evil, justice and injustice. The myths about me spring, of course, not from my "renown" alone, but from my attempts to speak in the same language of justice and injustice, addressing two shores divided by conflict but, like mankind itself, at one in their meaning and destiny.

It does sound suspicious. I'm sometimes guilty of trying to grasp the ungraspable and, as a wise man once said, "When you try to embrace all mankind, you sometimes forget your wife." My strength perhaps, but also my failing, is a greediness for life. My fear of not expressing myself on some topic makes me express myself at times too superficially. Leaping like a seismograph to the quivers of Earth's core, I'm often deaf to the silence. In general, we the poets of the atomic age too often substitute nervousness for spirituality.

I may have won the ear of many nations, but it's a mixed blessing. Readers are too despotic. Once in love with a poet for something, they expect it to appear again and again, forever. They interpret any change in a poet's character, and consequently in his poetry, not as a normal development but as a retreat from principle. There aren't even two readers alike in the world, and if they number in the hundred thousands how can you please them all? You shouldn't try. A writer who has won the public's interest is misguided if he thinks he'll be free in the end; he'll soon feel its spur and bridle on his flesh.

Not long ago a young teacher from Saratov came to me with this reproach. "All you do now is analyze and analyze," she said, "but you can't uplift the masses with analysis alone. They rally to calls and appeals."

When you're young it's easy enough to streak appeals across the sky like rockets. But as you get older you feel increasingly responsible for those traveling the road your rocket lights. What if you've led them wrong? You grow wary of making reckless appeals, and a sense of responsibility must be tempered above all with analysis and reflection. Relentless analysis alone, not childish shouting, embodies the true appeals.

Once someone lovingly retyped all eight volumes of my collected works as a birthday present. Full of anticipation and delight I lay down on the sofa to read. I was instantly aghast. The lines seemed so naïve and precocious, sometimes criminally so, and congested with slogans. It was too late to do anything. "The word's no sparrow; once it goes, it won't fly back." Since that time my relationship with paper has undergone considerable change. I've begun to fear her, although certainly not enough.

Before judging his age a writer must find the courage to judge himself. Pushkin was strong enough not only to write poems for the overthrow of autocracy but to say of himself, "And reading my own life with loathing, I tremble and curse." You musn't be misled by the sins your myth ascribes but look soberly through to the real failings beneath.

Clearly many of my poems have not withstood the test of time, but I secretly believe something of me will survive my stay on Earth. Something at least of my fits of spirit, I hope, even if screened by smoke, may influence the feelings of my descendants, restored to each other at last from the ice of estrangement. That done, it little matters if, hearing the velvety whistles of magnificent ships to come, they don't recall the hoarse voice of the mail boat.

No one can foretell the outcome of our lives. What then must we do?

> Live, and by the smallest measure
> Never step back from oneself,
> But be alive, fully alive,
> Alive and only, to the end.

B. PASTERNAK

(signed)

Yevgeny Yevtushenko

Translated by Anthony Kahn

A TRANSLATOR'S PREFACE

No translator is at heart either a traitor or a tailor. In approaching the work of another man his function is neither to stick a knife in the other man's throat nor to dress him up in the fashion of the times. No voice can really speak for another, only to, and in the process the truth at stake and the measure of success is the honesty of the interchange. Something—or someone—deeply felt, as Yevtushenko was by all of us who worked with him, comes in at the heart and goes out the same way, as little like an echo as two people saying, "I love you," to one another.

A person seeking the "real" Yevtushenko will never find him anyway, only an image shaped by one's own feeling for the world and the truth—the main concerns of Yevtushenko's poetry—changing, as it must for Yevtushenko himself, from one moment to the next. A poem, a "translation," an "adaptation," though more concrete, is itself merely a record of impressions felt, analyzed, integrated into a point of view.

Yevtushenko asked each of the poets involved in this project to assume the most demanding freedom: to translate only poems he liked; and to be fully himself in his work. For some of us that meant working on an intimate lyric, for others a narrative as fluid and far-flung as the Pechora. For everyone it meant riding the impulse the original voice set off, as long and in such a way as he wished. The result—these English adaptations—are interchanges between one poet and another.

At times translating Yevtushenko meant yielding, as it did for John Updike, to the public energy of the man and letting its curve "carry him into English combinations like nothing in our poetry since Whitman." For Geoffrey Dutton it often meant "listening to the ghosts" in Yevtushenko's verse, the voices that fed his own—Spanish, Armenian, German, Kirghiz, English, and Tajik—and feeling, through the music, the man's sharp hunger for the truth of his own experience. Richard Wilbur responded to the shock of a fresh voice speaking through traditional poetic forms, to the daring of the man, to the intimacy of his love for the world, to his public display of the most private moments. Dickey's Yevtushenko leapt from the page "ebullient, rapid-fire, devil-take-the-hindmost-missing-nothing," flashing on the world with intense, unbounded imagination, hoisting the "hell-with-it" to a power that transformed it into the deepest possible involvement with life-at-flow. Stanley Kunitz found joy in discovering "the other Yevtushenko, the one with the north-country child in him, the lyric one with his sense of roots and natural affections." Each poet in his own way returning to his Yevtushenko the life-enhancing quality the man evoked. Each poet answering poetry with poetry and responding as one can only to a contemporary whose voice still strikes the ear and whose eyes still cut across the table, as they did for Ferlinghetti, where the glasses are unclouded and the vodka in them clear.

Each of us has met Yevtushenko in person and in print, and each of us has honestly tried to honor the request of our Russian friend who wrote to us:

> Doubleday and Company is to publish a volume of my verse in English translation. I have compiled the collection myself. The publication of this book is, for me, a matter of principle.
>
> I would hope my poetry could be translated by some of the very best poets writing in English today, and so I turn to you with a request for your help. You are, I know, a busy man, but really and truly, if we the poets of this world won't lend one another a hand, what then will befall the rest of mankind? In return for your help I give my solemn word to "take revenge" and translate several of your own poems which you might choose for me. I grant you, of course, full freedom in your work, for I know well from my own experience that only a free and unrestricted translation can in any way claim to be poetry.
>
> Yours,
>
> YEVGENY YEVTUSHENKO

Anthony Kahn
Cambridge, Massachusetts
1971

STOLEN APPLES

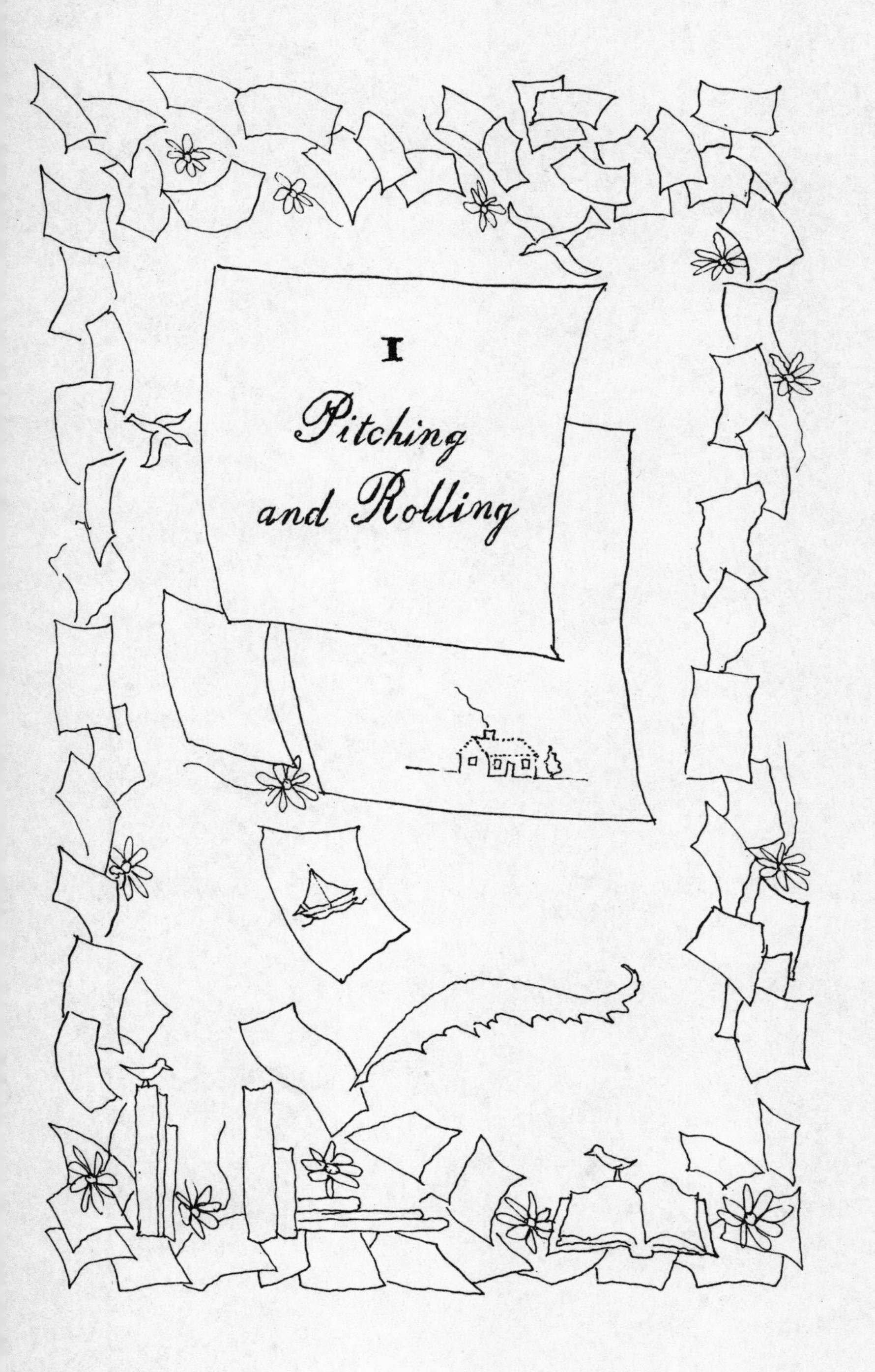
I
Pitching
and Rolling

THE HUT

And once again a fisherman's hut
opening to me late in the night,
suddenly as much a part of me
as the one along whose floor I used to crawl.

Quietly I lay down in the corner
as if it were my old lost place:—
that shaky, chinky floor,
whose every crack and knot I knew.

And I was home again, painfully at home,
amid the smells of fish and tobacco,
children, kittens, borscht,
fumes rising, purifying.

Already the room rocked with the fisherman's snores;
the children already had climbed into their bunks,
their teeth nibbling
on steamy pancakes.

Nobody but the housewife stirred,
washing, scrubbing.
A poker, a broom, a needle—
there must always be something in her hands.

4

Outside a storm was brewing on the Pechora:*
you could hear the river seethe.
"She's kicking up her heels," she said,
as if speaking of a coffee-colored cow.

A puff, blowing out the smoky lamp,
left the room to its own darkness.
I could hear the slap-slosh sound
of her laundry chores in the kitchen.

An old clock creaked in the night,
dragging the weight of history.
From the freshly laid kindling
a white fire broke and crackled.

And, full of wonder and fear,
untamed, from the shadows,
eight children's eyes gleamed
like eight sprays from your waters, Pechora.

They leaned out over their bunks
from an impossibly distant distance,
four little selves (myself)
watching a grown-up, me.

* Pechora: a Russian river over 1100 miles long, flowing south from Archangel, then west and north, widening steadily until it swings again north to its delta and the Pechora Sea. It is frozen from about November to April, when the thaw brings severe ice jams and flooding. [A.K.]

5

A silent prayer crossed my lips,
as I lay still, pretending to sleep.
And the kitchen noises stopped:
I heard the door squeak open.

And in this depth of solitude,
through the veil of this slumber,
I felt the touch of something
remembered from my childhood.

A sheepskin coat—that's what it was—
thrown on me snugly, shaggily, warmly;
and a moment later, from the kitchen tub,
the slapping of the clothes again.

I could almost see those hands dancing
through diapers, bedsheets, dungarees,
to the music of all our passions,
to the roar of world events.

Certainly more than one pretentious nonentity
had wormed his rotten way into eternity,
but only this recurring slap-slosh
struck me, in essence, as eternal.

6

And a teeming sense of fate
overwhelmed me,
like the exhalation of a hut
where life lies heavy on millions of women,

and where—who knows when?—
after the mastery has been won,
a million little selves (myself)
will watch a grown-up, me.

1964

TRANSLATED BY STANLEY KUNITZ
WITH ANTHONY KAHN

WOUNDED BIRD

to A. Voznesensky

Here to these wild stretches of the north
where the world first quacked and spawned,
I flew, a wounded bird, a drake,
and settled down on the Pechora.

From my covert by the woods
all my nerve-ends tingled
at the smell of ice-floes and seals,
the majesty, the vibrant breath, of ocean.

The sea was what I breathed,
it was sorrow I exhaled;
and the scattered buckshot in my blood
I gave as keepsake for Pechora,

my gift of leaden pellets
to the cold river bed. And trembled
and rose again and flapped my wings,
beating the air with a sudden power.

The winds rocked me gently,
adrift over mosses and bushes;
muskrats showed me the way, puffing down trails
behind their wet whiskers.

8

Through corridors of unplowed lands,
past flowering brakes and stands of hazelnut
tender-eyed deer bore me
on the velvet buds of their antlers.

Then the tussocks received me,
the tundra said, "Taste me,"
proffering its Iceland moss,
its cranberries sweetened through the winter.

And I—tuned to the clang of bolts and breechblocks—
knew that my life was precious,
only because you, shining, touched me,
caressed me, Pechora.

Sometime again, a mighty drake,
unrecognized by you, Pechora,
I'll fly over the north country,
flashing the brocade fan of my feathers.

And you will scan the arc of sky,
lost in the plumage and the flight,
forgetting that the gift was yours,
the saving gift, Pechora;

and how one spring you harbored me,
when unremittingly
that plumage spilled its tears of blood
into your light blue hem, Pechora.

1963

TRANSLATED BY STANLEY KUNITZ
WITH ANTHONY KAHN

MATING FLIGHT OF THE WOODCOCK

Shoulder your gun, be steady, sight.
With bill outstretched, needle-sharp,
the woodcock plunges out of the moon
straight toward you, darkening the moon.

He pitches, whistling on the wing,
down through the evening air. Tell me,
why is he drawn to you, as on a string,
why is your muzzle guided by a string?

Joy is the music of his fall.
Trembling, you hug your weapon tight.
Hunter, he is your unarmed double.
You are his doomed and wingless double.

Can you atone for winglessness
with a blast of wings? Squeeze out your shot:
but that's yourself in careless flight,
yourself you're shooting down in flight.

TRANSLATED BY STANLEY KUNITZ
WITH ANTHONY KAHN

GLASHA, BRIDE OF THE SEA

A Tale of the North Country

She knows the river, net and hook,
and hunts it deep as any.
Love opens her a petaled look:
"I couldn't care a penny!
You're better dead."
She shakes her head:
her angry earrings dance.
She walks in scarf and sarafans
she spins from Northern Light!
No other finger trains her hair
or teaches tress to toss and play,
no other ribbon winds her braid
but the river's wave!
She moves along the shore
and mends her nets. She beams
a leaping look beneath her brow
like salmons scale a stream!
I stood enchanted at the root
and dared a timid dream of fruit.

But tongues did roll in pub and spire
and toss about her name
and bandy it in crew and choir
and gossip she was tamed.
O!
    "Who bends the wind? Who drowns the rain?"
Mad I walked.
                    "It's all a joke!"
The townsmen puffed their pipes and spoke
me silent smoke.
"Who rings her finger? Who braids her hair?"
I faced northwest
and asked the air.

Suddenly up by my side
pops a tramp,
sprouted like a tundra toadstool
in the damp.
"Give a drink and get an answer
by and by," says he.
"I'll shed a secret on your saucer
like a sprig of tea." So,
he drains a glass and drains another
and when my money's dry,
"The icy ocean is her lover,"
he winks.
"And she's his bride."

I stood up fierce, my stormy fists
raged to pound his frame,
"They make a plaything of my pain
for fowl and fish to see,
the deep pike cackles in the river,
the high loon howls at me!"

Glasha busies at her boat,
tarring back and side,
and shows the sun her mended sail
stitched to leak no light.
I speak my heart:
"Above the wave
the fish leaps and the dipping drake
skims a hungry beak.
For your velvet look I'd lay
the tundra at your feet
and lullaby your tattered coat
to sleep in ermine sheets
and track the fishes' mating steps
from ocean dance to spawning pool
and catch a salmon in my net
rich with roe of pearls,
and trap you dreams you never dared
and what you wished of wildest fruit
to slake the travels of your boots
through salty sea and scale.
You tricked my lip upon your hook
and lure of flashing teeth,

and now I'm bluffed of coin and keep
and townsmen tell me, drunk and brief,
you're promised to the sea!"

Answers Glasha,
"I'm his bride.
Look at the river. Restless water
runs beneath the wave
and hastens to the greyer fathoms
where my lover waits. Today
I'll lift an oar and lure a breeze
to sail me, unannounced, to sea.
I'll drop beneath the cloudy night
and hug the thunder of his breast
till all is dark forgetfulness
and dreams of things that come and go
upon the sighing of a pillow
made of porpoises at rest.
I'll ask my age, I'll hear him say
that all my turns about the sun
were seventeen salmon in a wave
and seventeen fishscales on a blade.
In rolling thunder
and chilly light
he'll rumble me his answers
and speak to me of life.
Lad, your words won't win a wife
for all they'll ever say of life
when I have heard the sea!"

14

Her ship gained snowy sail at that,
cupped a breeze,
and drew her on a sharp tack
to the sea.
I whispered words I soon forgot
and turned with empty eyes from what
I might have had of life, but for the sea.
And felt the fact drop like a hook
that caught and drew a moan from me,
"What will I ever say of life
to ears that heard the sea?"

TRANSLATED BY ANTHONY KAHN

BALLAD ABOUT FALSE BEACONS

. . . and those far, elusive lights plunged the souls of seamen into darkness, offering them false hope . . .

From an ancient pilot's manual

We've been bewitched by countless lies,
by azure images of ice,
by false promises of open sky and sea,
and rescued by a God we don't believe.
Like coppers rattling from a beggar's plate
guiding lights have fallen on our days
and burned and died.

We've pressed our ship
a pilgrimage of nights toward such lights
as, always elusive, lured and tricked
the keel upon the rocks and ripped
the helmhold from the hand and lashed
the beggared palm to scraps.
Ice tightens at the bow and breath.
To dock, to drop the anchor to its rest,
to drift (a dream!) on waters quieted
and calmed. We can't. We're after a mirage.
(The whiskered walrus brays; the salt sea thaws.
Again, we're off!)
Raised on powdered milk, we'll have no faith
in beacons any longer, nor mistake
real for fake, or waking for a dream.
Beacons can't be trusted. Trust instead

the will of your own hand and head.
Again the captain waves his glass,
sights a beacon, turns and cries
"Helmsman! There's a beacon. Are you blind?"
But Helmsman, with the truer eye
thinks mutiny and grumbles,
"A mirage."

1964

TRANSLATED BY ANTHONY KAHN

PITCHING AND ROLLING

Here we go! We're RE-E-ELING!
The glass-framed instructions
rip off their nails.—
A Spidola record player bashes you in the head
with Doris Day.—
Borscht, lazing in the galley,
takes off straight up, splashing
madly—
A bay leaf from the borscht,
stuck to the ceiling, steams.
Reel on! buddy!
Sure; you'd like to catch hold of a bush or some grass
with your hands!
The cabin boy staggers.
The helmsman staggers.
The boatswain staggers.
I'm staggering—
The waves like wolfhounds—
You're just the same, Twentieth Century,
right-left
left-right
up-down
down-up—

Reeling!

All instructions shatter—

all the portraits smash to hell!

Faces are death white drawn wasted

under the stern, a

rat-like

screech

And all over the place it's dense with kasha

with downwind screams

nothing but pitching and rolling, staggering, curving
with the taste of sick stomach in your mouth.

Reeling!

A barrel jumps down the deck

throwing itself at people.
Hey, old buddies, we're in for it now

but keep it cool anyway.

Crawl out of your cabins, otherwise

it's *kaput* for us all.

Reeling . . .

But the eyes of the harpooner

a ringtailed roarer

are strained, and his forelock's standing straight up.
He makes a soundless sign to the sailors

and steals sideways

with a rope

to the flipped out barrel

and pitches himself like a cat

splitting open the crowd,

For he knows, you bastard pitch and roll, things can get rough—
He's learned by heart, right through his skin, his red head,

He's had it beat down through his skull:
Either you jump on the barrel
          or it'll jump all over you!
We're reeling!
                    But the barrel's still, it's no longer running
                                                  wild . . .
We're reeling!
                    Clear weather won't run off from us . . .
Reeling!
               We may be seasick, darkness in front of our eyes—
But we'll out-reel you
                              bad trip
                                             anyway . . .

TRANSLATED BY JAMES DICKEY
WITH ANTHONY KAHN

II
Doing the Twist
on Nails

THE INCENDIARY

You are completely free of affectation:
silent you sit, watchfully tense,
just as silence itself pretends to nothing
on a starless night in a fire-gutted city.

Consider that city—it is your past,
wherein you scarcely ever managed to laugh,
now raging through the streets, now sunk in self,
between your insurrections and your calms.

You wanted life and gave it all your strength,
but, sullenly spurning everything alive,
this slum of a city suffocated you
with the dreary weight of its architecture.

In it every house was shuttered tight,
in it shrewdness and cynicism ruled,
it never hid its poverty of spirit,
its hate for anyone who wasn't broken.

And so one night you burned it down
and ran for cover, frightened by the flames,
till chance produced me in your way, the one
you stumbled on when you were fugitive.

I took you in my arms, I felt you tremble,
as quietly your body clung to mine,
not knowing me or caring, but yet,
like an animal, grateful for my pity.

Together then we sallied . . . where did we go?
Wherever our eyes, in their folly, took us.
But intermittently you had to turn
to watch your past ominously burning.

It burned beyond control, till it was ashes.
And I remain tormented to this day
that you are drawn, as though enchanted,
back to that place where still the embers glow.

You're here with me, and yet not here.
In fact you have abandoned me. You glide
through the smoldering wreckage of the past,
holding aloft a bluish light in your hand.

What pulls you back? It's empty and gray there!
Oh the mysterious power of the past!
You never could learn to love it as it was,
but yet you fell madly in love with its ruins.

Ashes and embers must be magnets too.
How can we tell what potencies they hold?
Over what's left where once she set her fire
the incendiary cries like a little child.

TRANSLATED BY STANLEY KUNITZ
WITH ANTHONY KAHN

□ □ □

Damp white imprints dog the feet;
snowbound trolley, snowbound street.
Her tip of glove to lip and cheek,
"Goodby." Go.
Deathly, into soaring snow
and stillness, as expected, go.
A turn:
            the plunge to the metro.
A blare of lights. A melting hat.
I stand, am spun in drafts, see black
take the tunnel, train, and track,
sit and wait as others sat,
touch cold marble, chill my hand
and, heavy-hearted, understand
that nothing ever really happened,
ever would, ever can.

1956

TRANSLATED BY ANTHONY KAHN

MASHA

A girl goes along the seashore
blushing and shy
a tide rising in her
a woman rising in her

She takes off her shoes by the sea
and steps into it as into music
And she understands everything
though she doesn't understand a thing

Reason and rashness mixed—
A keen glance through us
and then again withdrawn—
All this is Masha—
a serious wide-eyed being

And the roof of my mouth goes dry
when her slender boyish legs
heedless of some grown-up's opinion
bear her helplessly to me

And on the wet sand by an old boat
with growing confidence I kiss
all that Masha's arms are—from elbow
to the rose petals of her nails

I put on my snorkel gear
and Masha swims somewhere above me
I search for Masha through the glass
as if drunk among the crabs and flowers

And I see in the bright green gloaming
in a bank of clouds above the underwater ridge
her legs like white stalks
fluttering submerged

And I swim and swim in the underwater thickets
and I swim, my fins thatching the water,
and I'm unhappy because I'm happy
and then happy because I'm unhappy

What can I say? Tell Mother not to worry
Masha I'll do you no harm
Masha I ask so little of you
and yet so much—just that you exist—

In meditations on death and eternity
gripped by hope and melancholy
I look through your slender little heart
as through a transparent pebble in the sea

1958

TRANSLATED BY LAWRENCE FERLINGHETTI
WITH ANTHONY KAHN

LET'S NOT . . .

Let's not . . .
Everything's ghostly—
the blank windows watching,
the snow reddening behind the stoplights of the cars.
Let's not . . .
Everything's ghostly, lost in mist,
like a garden in March emptied of men and women,
paraded by
shadows.
Let's not . . .
I stand by a tree,
not speaking, undeceiving,
facing
the double glare of the headlights,
and with a quiet hand touch
but do not break
the tender icicle imprisoning a twig.
Let's not . . .
I see you in the sleepy, reeling trolley
with spectral Moscow rocking in the window,
your cheek propped on a child's wool mitten,
thinking of me with a woman's rancor.

Let's not . . .

You'll be a woman soon enough, subtle and worn,
hungry for praise, for the balm of a caress;
it will be March again,
a callow boy will whisper in your ear,
your head will whirl inconsolably.
Let's not . . .
For both your sakes,
don't stroll with him down the slippery paths,
don't place
your insubordinate hands
upon his shoulders,
even as I do not place them today.
Let's not . . .
Oh disbelieve, like me, in the ghostly city.
Be spared
from waking in the wasteland,
terrified.
Say: "Let's not . . ."
bending your head,
as I this moment
say
"Let's not . . ."
to you . . .

1960

TRANSLATED BY STANLEY KUNITZ
WITH ANTHONY KAHN

ASSIGNATION

No, no! Believe me!
I've come to the wrong place!
I've made a god-awful mistake! Even the glass
In my hand's an accident
and so's the gauze glance
Of the woman who runs the joint.
"Let's dance, huh?
You're pale . . .
Didn't get enough sleep?"
And I feel like there's no place
To hide, but say, anyway, in a rush
"I'll go get dressed . . .
No, no . . . it's just
That I ended up out of bounds . . ."
And later, trailing me as I leave:
"This is where booze gets
you . . .
What do you mean, 'not here'? *Right* here! Right here every time!
You bug everybody, and you're so satisfied
With yourself about it. Zhenichka,
You've got a problem."

I shove the frost of my hands
Down my pockets, and the streets around are snow,
Deep snow. I dive into a cab. Buddy, kick this thing! Behind
the Falcon
There's a room. They're supposed to be waiting for me there.
She opens the door
but what the hell's wrong with her?
Why the crazy look?
"It's almost five o'clock.
You sure you couldn't have come a little later?
Well, forget it. Come on in. Where else could you go now?"
Shall I explode
with a laugh
or maybe with tears?
I tell you I was scribbling doggerel
but I got lost someplace.
I hide from the eyes. Wavering I move backwards:
"No, no! Believe me! I've come to the wrong place!"
Once again the night
once again snow
and somebody's insolent song
and somebody's clean, pure laughter.
I could do with a cigarette.
In the blizzard Pushkin's demons flash past
And their contemptuous, bucktoothed grin
Scares me to death.

And the kiosks
And the drugstores
and the social security offices
Scare me just as much . . .
No, no! Believe me! I've ended up
In the wrong place again . . .
It's *horrible* to live
And even more horrible
not to live . . .
Ach, this being home-
less
Like the Wandering Jew . . . Lord! Now I've gotten myself
Into the wrong century
wrong epoch
geologic era
wrong
number
The wrong place again
I'm wrong
I've got it wrong . . .
I go, slouching my shoulders like I'd do
if I'd lost some bet,
and Ah, I know it . . . everybody knows
it . . .
I can't pay off.

TRANSLATED BY JAMES DICKEY
WITH ANTHONY KAHN

THE SNOW WILL BEGIN AGAIN

The snow will begin again, falling, falling,
and in its canvas I will read
the image of my youth again, calling
me wherever it may lead.

And it will lead me by the hand to the mystery
of someone's shadow, the tap of feet,
drawing me into the old, old conspiracy
of the lights, the trees, the blizzard in the street.

And those Moscow streets, the Mokhovayas,
the Stretenka, it will seem to me,
it will seem to me I still have not been young yet
but am touching the possibility.

And the vortex of night will start whirling, whirling,
and I will be funneled into wrong,
and my youth I have been following will be curtained
off by snow, nothing will belong.

But suddenly under the impartial sunstream
all her make-up is there to see,
like a gypsy bitch who has rubbed her orgasm against me
my youth will clear off and abandon me.

I will start over again, and change my life's pattern,
will put my naïveté to shame,
and gloomily will hold out my neck and attach
myself, like a stray dog, to a chain.

But the snow will begin again, falling, falling,
everything turning round like a spindle,
and my youth like a gypsy girl will be calling
again to me outside my window.

And the snow will begin again, falling, falling,
and I will gnaw my way through the chain,
and my life like a snowball will be rolling
towards a girl's fur boots again.

TRANSLATED BY GEOFFREY DUTTON
WITH IGOR MEZHAKOFF-KORIAKIN

I FELL OUT OF LOVE WITH YOU

I fell out of love with you—what a banal denouement,
just as banal as life, just as banal as death is.
Let me snap the string of this intolerable love-song,
smash the guitar in two—why force a comedy!

Only the pup, shaggy little monster, cannot understand
why you and I make complex every simple thing.
As soon as I let him in, he runs to your door and scratches,
but he scratches at my door every time you let him in.

Really, you could go mad, dashing about like this.
Sentimental dog, I know you're immature,
but I refuse to become a sentimentalist.
To drag out the last act is to prolong the torture.

To be sentimental is not a weakness but a crime—
when you soften again, again promise reconciliation,
and groaning attempt to stage a show, yet another time,
under the insipid name of "Love's Salvation."

You should start saving love right at the beginning
from those passionate "Forevers!", those childish "Nevers!"
"Do not make promises!"—the trains were bellowing.
"Do not make promises!"—mumbled the telephone wires.

Half-cracked branches of trees and the smoke-smudged sky
were warning us, so ignorant in our conceit,
that optimism is merely untaught simplicity,
that hopes are always safer when they are not too great.

It is kinder to stay quite sober and soberly weigh the worth
of the links before putting them on—that's the creed of the chain,
not to promise heaven but at least to give the earth,
not to promise until death do part but at least give life again.

When you are in love it is kinder not to keep on saying "I love you."
How hard it is later, from the same mouth, to hear it destroyed
in words that are void of truth, in sneers, gibes that mock you,
making the world we had thought perfect seem false and void.

It is better not to promise. Love is something one can't realize,
why then lead someone into deceit as to the altar?
Of course the vision is wonderful, until it flies.
It is kinder not to love when you know love has no future.

Our poor dog keeps on whining, enough to drive us to madness,
with his paws scratching now on your door, now on my door.
I no longer love you; for that I do not ask forgiveness.
I did love you; that is what I ask forgiveness for.

TRANSLATED BY GEOFFREY DUTTON
WITH IGOR MEZHAKOFF-KORIAKIN

□ □ □

In aircraft, the newest, inexorable models,
I was zooming up like passion,
Flying from hope to hope,
Killing this one, then that one.

But hope was in the middle,
Beyond this flinging and the take-off markers,
Like a seal on a chip of ice
With its sad muzzle lifted.

I pressed my lip to my lip
On the bitter sweetness of flight
Candy, but got scared quick, bursting with a double-love
Like an empty aerogram.

Tenderness called me like the void
Into the rustling of fallen-off clothes,
But the touch of any hope plunged me
Again into hopelessness.

I sped back and forth in a sick panic,
With a hard-hit mask of a face,
With a mind split two ways,
Both ways false.

Look: once through the whirling of the earth
I saw from a taxi window
That a center-split pine
Moaned by the road like a lyre.

So you see it wasn't *that* crazy
That, a flying Wandering Jew, I
Involved the sky—right?—I said
The sky, in my private life.

And the straight routes of the flights slice through
The downpours, now here, now there—you almost want to cut them,
Like the strings of a groaning lyre
Between two hopeless hopes.

TRANSLATED BY JAMES DICKEY
WITH ANTHONY KAHN

DOING THE TWIST ON NAILS

When you throw your dancing shoes out, back over your shoulder,
And lose yourself, you find yourself twisting on the stage,
dancing,
dancing,
dancing—
let that pink boy whip you around—I can tell you:
Life doesn't dance this way—
That way dances death.
Thighs
shoulders
breasts:
they're all in it!
Inside you, dead drunk,
wheezes of air are dancing
Somebody else's ring
dances on your hand,
And your face by itself
doesn't dance at all
Flying, lifelessly, above all the body's life
Like a mask taken off your dead head.
And this stage—
is only one part of that cross
On which they once
crucified Jesus;

The nails shot through to the other side, and you began
To dance on them,
sticking out.
And you dance
On the nails
nails
On scandals red as rust
on the thorn-points of tears: Listen,
Because I once loved you, tiresomely, gloomily,
I also hammered the crooks of my nails
into this stage.
Ah, bestial, beastly music,
do you keep on getting stronger?
No one can see the blood
ooze from your foot-soles—
To wash the steps with clean water,
I'd rather you'd do it, Mary Magdalene,
not Jesus.
I'll wash all their days, their yesterdays, not like a brother would
For a sister,
but like a sister for a sister.
I'll kneel down and pick up your feet
And hold them quietly, and with kisses try to do something
About their wounds.

TRANSLATED BY JAMES DICKEY
WITH ANTHONY KAHN

THE INEXPRESSIBLE

I want what's inexpressible!
Impudent, I play with fire without a queen

My queen-reason is under the knight's hooves
What joy to lose to the fire!

What flaming in the uncombed night
From slender you, as from a candle!

How you've fired-up
The idea of sin!

I writhe but the cry of my flesh is bliss
The heretic is already freed by the fire

Gul'ripshi
New York Paris Madrid in flames
And someone dear to me burns in them

But if from the heretic's fire
The flame leaps to some poor bastard's roof

All the heretic burns for
Shall be forever damned to hell

For truth, when you burn down the scene
of someone nearby,
Is no longer truth but a lie.

TRANSLATED BY LAWRENCE FERLINGHETTI
WITH ANTHONY KAHN

□ □ □

Light died in the hall . . . Yet while, upon the boards,
Darkness arose and played the only role,
There poured through all my veins, in icy chords,
The chill of an inaudible chorale.

I knew that there, prepared for the prologue, seen
By none, perhaps, but the wide eye of God,
Like a sliver of the darkness, like a lean
Shade among shadows, slim and alive, you stood.

I had not God's high vision, yet within,
Like the voice of God, I felt the music rise,
And I saw, not with my sight but with my skin,
As with a thousand small, concerted eyes,

And there, in the dark, in the intermittencies
Of someone's breathing, the dense transparencies
Of the incorporeal shadows, I discovered
With a wild guess, and could in rapture tell
That point, apart from paradise or hell,
Where, waiting for its flame, a candle hovered.

44

And you were kindled, and the light re-uttered,
And the chaos of strange blackness was no more,
And only a little golden forelock fluttered
Before me, like a wind-whipped tongue of fire.

TRANSLATED BY RICHARD WILBUR
WITH ANTHONY KAHN

STOLEN APPLES

Fences careened in the storm;
we stole through the bitter shadows
like thieving children warmed
by shirtfuls of stolen apples.

The apples wanted to spill;
to bite them was scandalous.
But we loved one another
and that fact redeemed us.

Secluding the criminal twins
in a cosmos of dirty waves,
the snug cottage whispered,
"Be brave and love . . . be brave . . ."

The cottage's owner, an ex-
soccer hero, from his photo
dim on the glimmering mantel,
urged, "Be bold . . . plunge through . . ."

So, pivoting and twisting,
we burst through the penalty zone,
slipped past the last defender,
and billowed the nets of the goal!

Rest period. Above us, dust
flickered; we seemed to dream,
small soccer shoes vibrated
on an invisible field.

"Play," each mote insisted,
"Play, but play earnestly.
The earth's heavy globe is a speck
Like us, essentially."

We played again; we kicked.
The game perhaps was stupid
but we did love one another
and that felt splendid.

Drugged by its roaring, the sea
mumbled of something profound
but then a golden fish, your bang,
splashed upon your brow,

and I was unconcerned to know
that once on the storm's other side,
for all my bravura folly,
I'd sink back with the tide.

Let slander pursue me;
love isn't for the feeble.
The odor of love is the scent
not of bought but of stolen apples.

What matters the watchman's shout
when, wrapped in the sea's far hiss,
I can cushion my head between
two salty apples I've filched.

TRANSLATED BY JOHN UPDIKE
WITH ANTHONY KAHN

□ □ □

I dreamed I already loved you.
I dreamed I already killed you.

But you rose again; another form, but you,
A girl on the little ball of the earth,
Naïve simplicity, curve-necked
On that early canvas of Picasso,
And prayed to me with your ribs
"Love me," as though you said, "Don't push me off."

I'm that played-out, grown-up acrobat,
Hunch-backed with senseless muscles,
Who knows that advice is a lie,
That sooner or later there's falling.

I'm too scared to say I love you
Because I'd be saying I'll kill you.

For in the depths of a face I can see through
I see the faces—can't count them—
Which, right on the spot, or maybe
Not right away, I tortured to death.

You're pale from the mortal balance. You say
"I know everything; I was all of them.
I know you've already loved me.
I know you've already killed me.
But I won't spin the globe backwards
We're on: Love again, and then kill again."

Lord, you're young. Stop your globe.
I'm tired of killing. I'm not a damn thing but old.

You move the earth beneath your little feet,
You fall, "Love me."
It's only in those eyes—so similar, you say
"This time don't kill me."

TRANSLATED BY JAMES DICKEY
WITH ANTHONY KAHN

THE OLD HOUSE

The old house was swaying, composing a chorale with its creaking,
and the creaking of the chorale was a funeral service sung for us.
This house of many creaks could sense that secretly
you and I were slowly mingling with its dust.

"Do not die yet"—the words were in the neighing from the meadows,
in the long howl of the dogs, the incantation of the pines,
but side by side, each to the other, we were dying already,
and that is the same as is generally known as dying.

And yet what a yearning to live! The woodpecker tapping the
pine-log,
a tame hedge-hog running about in the mushrooms near the house,
and the night floating like a shaggy-coated, wet, black dog,
holding a star like a water lily in its mouth.

Through the window the darkness was breathing the scent of wet
raspberries,
and behind my back—my back had eyes that never missed!—
my beloved was sleeping with Platonov's *Fro,** worn out with worries,
as peacefully as with a newly discovered sister.

* A novel by the modern Russian writer Platonov (1899–1951). His story, *Fro* (first published in 1936), depicts a woman in love.

I lay thinking of the dull imperfection of marriages,
of the dishonorableness of us all—traitors, dissemblers.
For I loved you as much as forty thousand brother-warriors,
and was destroying you as if they all were enemies.

What good thing then has all my fiery declaiming stirred,
if, scattering myself from the stage, making the clichés roll,
I wanted to give happiness to the whole world
and found I could not give it to one living soul?

Yes, you're a different person now. The tightening of your eyelids
is angry and merciless. Bitter your ridicule of other people.
And yet, who but we ourselves make those we love
into such creatures, loving them is beyond our power?

Yes, we were dying. But there was something that would not let me
be completely convinced that you and I did not exist.
Love still existed there. Love could still draw breath
and mist the mirror held in front of her weak lips.

Swaying and creaking amongst the nettles the old house survived,
volunteering to lend us its endurance.
We were dying in it, but we were still alive.
We loved each other, this was the proof of our existence.

Some time in the future—God do not let me, do not let me!
when I will fall out of love with you, and really die,
my flesh will stir in the darkness and secretly laugh at me:
"You're alive!"—it will whisper in the deceptive fever of the night.

But in the drive of passion, wiser, though sadly mortified,
suddenly I will understand that the voice of the flesh tells lies,
and I will say to myself: "I fell out of love. I died.
But once upon a time I loved and was alive."

TRANSLATED BY GEOFFREY DUTTON
WITH IGOR MEZHAKOFF-KORIAKIN

INCANTATION

Think of me on spring nights
and think of me on summer nights,
think of me on autumn nights
and think of me on winter nights.
Though I'm not there, but somewhere gone,
far from your side, as if abroad,
stretch yourself on the long cool sheet,
float on your back, as in the sea,
surrendering to the soft slow wave,
with me, as with the sea, utterly alone.

I want nothing on your mind all day.
Let the day turn everything upside down,
besmudge with smoke and flood with wine,
distract you till I fade from view.
All right, think of anything by day,
but in the night—only of me alone.

Over the locomotive whistles, over
the wind, ripping the clouds to shreds,
listen to me, for pity's sake:
show me again, in the narrow room,
your eyes half-shut with ecstasy and pain,
your palms pressing your temples till they ache.

54

I beseech you—in the stillest stillness,
or when the rain patters on your roof,
or the snow sparks on your windowpanes,
and you lie between sleep and waking—
think of me on spring nights
and think of me on summer nights,
think of me on autumn nights
and think of me on winter nights.

1960

TRANSLATED BY STANLEY KUNITZ
WITH ANTHONY KAHN

BLACK AND WHITE

To Lannie MacNulty

I

Senegal,
I dive to the very dregs of the pubs
                                        safe from toadies and narks,
with black circles
round my eyes
          after crazy nights of crashing around in the dark.
I spit
on all those hypocrites splashing on the surface—
                                                  those and these,
and I swim
amongst the underwater plants,
          the violet-shimmering bodies.
Wailing,
two mulatto girls shake on the stage
          and under them the earth thrashes.
Their gaze
is greedy as sea anemones
          inside the tentacles of their eyelashes.
But, caught through
the smoke-fumes scarce swaying
          I am drawn across years and hours

by your two
brown eyes,
like two truthful underwater flowers.
We are bound
together, children of fated, Shakespearean feuding and
hating,
the White House
the Grey House*
we've forced our way through your nets
to our very own meeting.
We're on the run,
they're after us,
with bloodhounds, sirens, bedlam's blare.
We have flung
ourselves at the feet of our one true mother—
eternity, stroking our hair.
Lannie—
you've landed
beside me like a doe
who has jumped over seas, rockets and
destroyers.
Where is the banned
border zone between us?
Only my skin and yours.
So try
to jump over even this border
and give me your open lips to drink right down.

* Yevtushenko's note: "The Grey House" is what the progressive youth of South Africa call their Parliament House.

If we two lie
skin pressed into skin
    we will make ourselves one.
O night,
  scream!
Drunken mobs are exploding inside you
    like an atomic nightmare.
Knives gleam
and flicker like maddened fish
    over the seaweed of hair.
Scraped back,
chairs take off into the air,
    brass knuckles scrunch into guts.
Like maniacs
whites stab blacks,
    blacks whites,
      and the yellow hack them all to bits.
Over bellowing cattle
and above the brawling,
    as if icy Biblical clouds rang,
hail rattling,
the cocktail shaker dances
    in the barman's tenacious passionless hands.
The switch-blade twists
through ribs, the cosh smashes home
    while the barman stands above the crunch of
        bones and claws—

God exists!—
the barman whips up our souls
into a cocktail ordered
centuries before.
Over thieves
over beasts
I cautiously take hold of your white hand.
We have each other.
"Aren't you frightened?" I ask with my eyes,
and your eyes answer: "No, I'm not frightened."
What do I care
for the malice of all the world's bandits,
or its coming doom,
if through the glare
of this horrible brawl
a face
is coming to me?
What is the cause
of this brawl?
Why should we care!
And maybe, all these knives
draw us
together
to press one to the other
in this maelstrom of nights.
What is love?
It is you, and it is I
over the brass-knuckles, the shots,
the assaults on existence.

What is love?
It is the eternal OVER
the throat-cutting of races, prejudices,
systems.
What is love?
It is the eternal OUTSIDE.
It's outside all fights, all sorts of brawls,
it's the union of Juliet and Romeo.
What is love?
"Aren't you frightened?"—the question with the eyes,
and the eyes' answer "No."

II

I came to see you off
with my two dark helpless hands—
not laden with flowers.
My Irish girl, farewell for ever . . .
But maybe?
Do you understand . . . ?
Goodbye, until we meet again . . .
Your name remains safe with me
to my last hour,
sacred,
Lannie.
If only we could see each other in this world
at least once more . . .

Goodbye, until we meet again!
"Ladies and gentlemen,
the aircraft for Paris
ready for departure!"
On a conveyor belt
suitcases swim
as if along a grey river to nowhere,
into the Caravelle.
We hold each other tight
lost like savages
in the hullabaloo
of speculators in
hashish,
ideas,
prostitutes,
and
even us two.
We are powerless, you and I,
and maybe we are just infantile,
and spineless?
There are handcuffs on my hands
and shackles on my ankles,
the only difference—
they don't clank.
I'm giving you away
and you are giving me away—
whoever may win
we are running away.

The handcuffs on your hands
show through
your white skin
cutting their way.
We are prisoners of our age,
prisoners of our governments and of our race.
Everywhere
there are fetters.
Of real freedom, for you or for us,
there is no trace.
Only
a few minutes,
then the python,
having set free his collapsing victim,
claps on
his coils again.
What is love?
Only a minute of freedom.
Then
a relapse
to worse pain.
People do not have rights
beyond the ancient right to suffer,
but even in this
the coils of our era
do not offer
us this
mean choice.

This age has squeezed our souls,
and, teasing us with illusions of freedom,
breaks them brutally.
If he who is trapped in the coils
can't have aeons of freedom,
then take
a minute!
And afterwards—
you can hang me,
skin me by slow degrees,—
just as you need!
But first give me the right
to suffer as I please,
just as I please!
Let us suffer once more
if once more I can have what you can give—
then farewell, again!
We think—does that mean we live?
No, we suffer, that means we live,
to share hell again!

TRANSLATED BY GEOFFREY DUTTON
WITH IGOR MEZHAKOFF-KORIAKIN

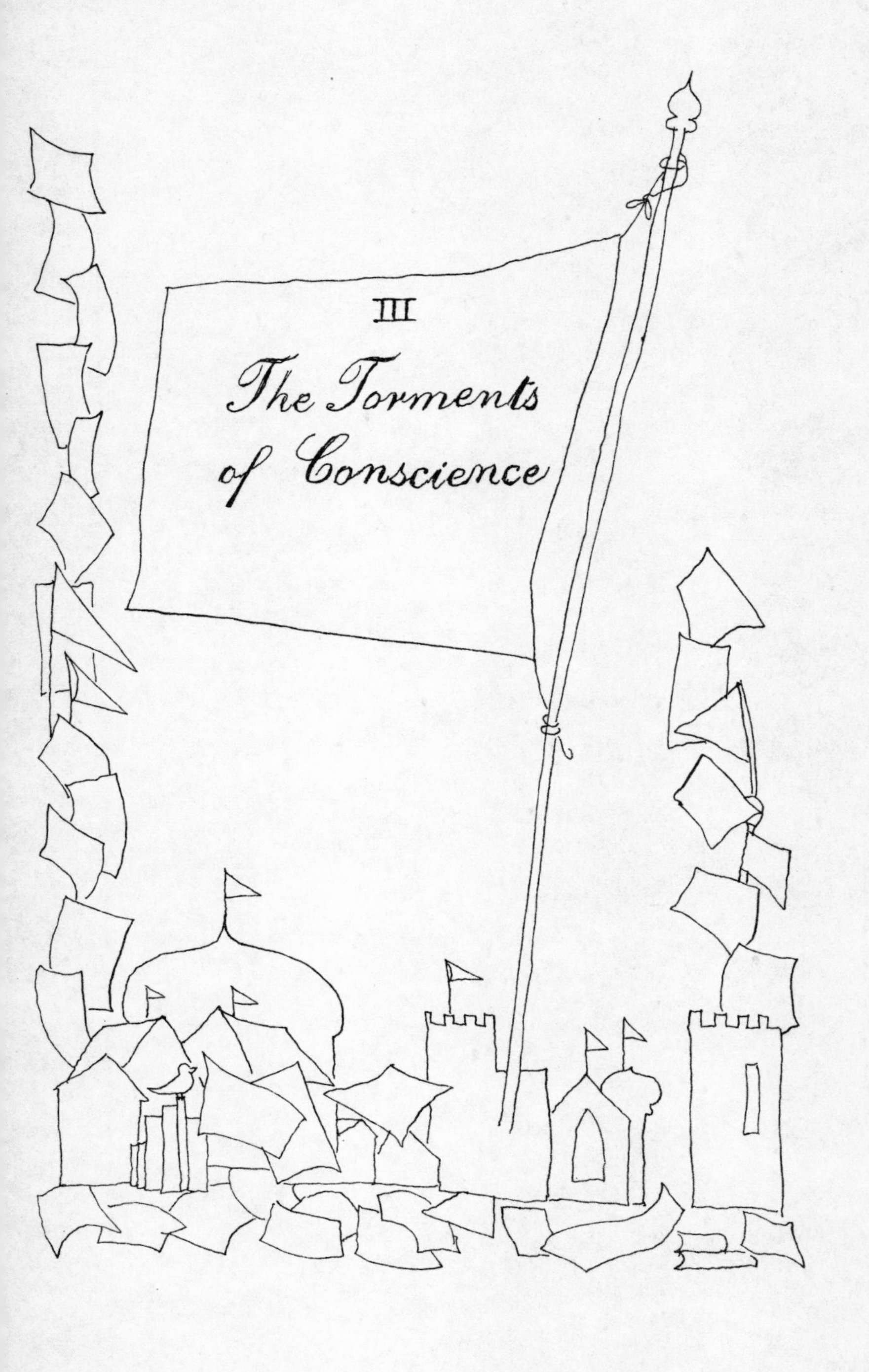
III
The Torments of Conscience

COWS

Stockinged in the river's slime,
the cattle coming slow.
This I remember. Precisely, though,
I can't say when.

Cow coats dimmed the earth and drew
a low hem on the hill.
The year was maybe forty-one,
or forty-two.

Burdocked hides, dusty brains
limping through a dream of grain.
Quiet schoolboys led the lean
beef to the train.

Weary too, I walked in back
to close the ranks, my horsetroop hat
a dome bleached white but for the black
memory of a star.

Ah cows, ah cows,
you dipped your pale horns down
into the meadows
like crowns,

and softly spoke and sadly rubbed
the shrubs against your hips
or lifted heads whose silent lips
spilled flowers.

Uneasily the calloused hands
marked by sledge and vein
stripped the throats of string and bell,
led the cattle to the train.

And coat to coat they drank and sang
until a far light spoke.
The cars began to creak and move
in steam and smoke.

White broke upon the darkened door:
a frightened calf with human eyes,
a child's face, and at his side,
the butcher.

Pressed to the cloth, bewildered eyes
that thought the speeding grass and wood
had fled their roots, bewildered eyes
but, like Yesenin's,* blue.

1960

TRANSLATED BY ANTHONY KAHN

* Sergei Yesenin (1895–1925). Peasant-born and, as he described himself, "the last poet of wooden Russia," he welcomed the Revolution as a spiritual event sure to inaugurate the peasant millennium. In the early 1920s he led a Bohemian life in the capital, drank heavily, married and divorced Isadora Duncan, grew disenchanted with himself and the Revolution, and committed suicide in Leningrad.

□ □ □

But only the divine word . . .
Pushkin

Poetry gives off smoke
but it doesn't die out.
It acts kind of crazy, flutteringly,
when it chooses us.
This fellow's no fool,
sucking tranquillizers,
toting in a little briefcase
a boiled beet-root.
Right now he'd like a mousse
or baba au rhum,
but the Muse—
some kind of Muse!—
grabs him
by the scruff of the neck!
Thoughts drill a hole in his forehead,
and he's mislaid the spoon—
and he's a giant! Socrates, for the Lord's sake . . .
in an Oblomov dust-jacket. O.K. . . .
he's no Apollo—
he's puny and ugly,
skinny: he's like a golden mushroom,
unsteady . . .
transparent.

But suddenly some sort of whistling
is in his ears, and then . . .
a period!
And like a slugger's hook
across the chops of the ages,
a line!
And there
an insane little bird
falls off its feet,
a crazy rag-picker,
drunk,
a kind of society clown. But something gives her the word
and—
like branches in winter,
God rings from within, and her eyelids turn
to marble.
And here's a bum
a shaman,
really—
from among the lunatics!
Pour him champagne,
bring him
women, not rum cakes!
Suddenly an order from within
will come through sternly, and he's the instant
voice of the people, damned near
Savonarola!

Poetry acts kind of strange, it flutters
when it chooses us.
And it has no mercy, either,
afterwards. It stamps "Pure Souls"
on us . . . but who's the judge?

Yes,

for the horse-blinkered multitudes we're "decadents,"
but for our*selves,* we ourselves are . . . are . . .
well, yes! Redemption!

TRANSLATED BY JAMES DICKEY
WITH ANTHONY KAHN

IN THE WAX MUSEUM AT HAMBURG

Full of blocky majesty,
arrogant, dock-tailed,
German princes glower
at the Russian communist.
All the presidents,
chancellors
in their different kinds of gut-
meanness look darkly out
each his own kind,
his caste, and all their crooked
vulgarity is in that.
These are the wounders
of life. They warped it,
suffocated it, and so
they're immortalized here—
or, no,
they're waxed.
In the midst of these grown fat
these greasy fools, and emaciated, malicious monsters
how did you fall,
Schiller?
How about you,
Mozart?

You should have landed
in luminous meadows;
Should have come down among
deep-woods flowers.
But you're here—
my old buddies,
Enemies—
the whole damned lot. The enemies' looks are trying
To kill me, but it's not so bad,
This not being liked
by Bismarck, and surely not
By Hitler.
I keep looking, and gradually I see,
Among them like fatal ghosts,
the shaped, candle-stick figures
Of enemies
still living. Yes. Still living.
There's one
premier,
There's another one, and *he's*
No shining example
and he's not either.
But maybe they *are*
examples: yes,
but of the mean, the cruel,
the phony . . .
I'd like to get them here *themselves,*
Into the wax museum
by the scruff of the neck,
By the seat of the britches!

It'd be great
To arrange 'em according to their crimes—
And let 'em be buried in wax
as ugly as *they* are!
I tell you, the wax museum is wild
For more bums and bastards!
Me,
I'm sick and tired of 'em! Sons-of-bitches
Have been lying to us too damned long!
It's time to drown 'em alive—
Right! In wax!
Let wax plaster their mouths
Shut, let it stop their hands
where they are
and let them stand
Still
still
very still
And dead
like good little children
very still
very
Obedient.
Right here and now I'm coming out with my
program
For revolution! I call on
EVERYONE! Drag 'em from their platform,
And while you're doing it, laugh and whistle
As loud as you can!
Go *get* 'em,
People! Let's have a little more
Pure rage!

It's time to pull down all this trash
From their easy chairs
like pulling nails and being crazy
About pulling nails!
It's time, under hot bright lights,
To drag down out of their balconies
This collection of stupid faces
Like carp from scummy green pools.
It's time, it's really time at last
To get rid of junk like this!
Into the wax museum
Of liars
with these priests of a lousy temple!
People!
SAY IT!
Don't clam up!
Into the wax museum
With all heads of state
Who're headless!
And if somebody lies, even
if he does it in a new way,
then
Stuff his gullet with wax!
Into the wax museum!
There's still a lot of bullshit around,
And plenty of liars . . . Hey,
BEES! Get off your ass!
Wax, little brothers! We need it!

TRANSLATED BY JAMES DICKEY
WITH ANTHONY KAHN

THE DEPTH

to V. Sokolov

The bellow of a steamer in the morning
woke the coniferous distances,
and we stood on deck,
spellbound by the Angara,
gazing straight to the river-floor,
where the painted rocks gleamed
through a bright green dimension.
We could not trust our eyes.
It seemed, at times, in our passage
that we could reach over the side
and with our fingertips touch bottom;
for depth could not be gauged
in that transparency of water.
Of course I know that danger lurks
in the unturbidity of the wave,
and that the clearest purling stream
may be the shallowest.
But deepness isn't all.
I wouldn't give a tinker's dam
for a stupid stagnant pond
where the eye sees nothing plain.

Let me be like the flow of a river
obliquely struck by sunset glow,
as deep as measureless,
with each
            small pebble
                        shining through!

1952

TRANSLATED BY STANLEY KUNITZ
WITH ANTHONY KAHN

THE TORMENTS OF CONSCIENCE

to D. Shostakovich

We live, dying is not our business,
shame is another lost episode,
but like an unseen madonna, conscience
is standing at every crossroad.

And her children and her grandchildren,
the torments of conscience—strange torments—
with vagrant's crutch and bag are wandering
a world which is everywhere dishonest.

From one gate once more to the next gate,
once again from doorstep to doorstep,
chanting like the old Russian beggars,
they travel with God for their heart's help.

Surely it was they who always haunted
the serfs, tapping with one finger
secretly on their windows, and who pounded
with their fists in the palaces of the Tsars?

Surely they hurried off dead Pushkin
on a sledge in the snow from a black sky,
it was they who drove Dostoievsky to prison,
it was they who whispered to Tolstoy: "Fly!"

The executioners understood it thus:
"He who torments himself is a troublemaker.
Torments of conscience—this is dangerous!
Conscience itself must be liquidated!"

But like the clanging of an alarm bell
rattling their houses at night time,
torments of conscience—terrible—
frightened the executioners with their crimes.

For even the guardians of injustice,
who abandoned all honor long ago,
may no longer know the meaning of conscience,
but the torments of conscience they do know.

And if in this wide world where no one,
no one is guiltless, someone has heard
within himself the cry "What have I done?"
then something can be done with this world.

I do not believe in the prophets construing
the coming of the Second or the Thousandth Rome,
I believe in the words "What are you doing?"
in "What are *we* doing?" bitterly spoken.

And on the slippery edge of lost faith
I am kissing your dark hands,
for you alone are my last faith,
torments of conscience--fierce torments!

1966

TRANSLATED BY GEOFFREY DUTTON
WITH IGOR MEZHAKOFF-KORIAKIN

IN MEMORY OF AKHMATOVA

I

Two ages ours—and gone. How could we weep?
The very thought was dry. Alive,
she was beyond belief.
How could she die?

Gone like a nightsong, feathers
dipped through garden air
to a dim branch, as if forever
gone to Petersburg from Leningrad.

The parted times, the scattered days
regroup within her hazy light.
If Pushkin is our sun, surely she
is our White Night.

Beyond the give and take of breath,
the struggle in the mind of death
and immortality, between
the future and the past, she lies.

The past streamed softly by her grave:
proud grey ladies, lifting faces
shocked in silver, wearing bonnets
of another age.

Yes, time had dimmed that beauty, prized
highly by a Russia that had been,
but, lamps of kindliness, their eyes
still danced against the wind.

And, shoulders still too weak for worlds,
the future comes with molten eyes:
schoolboys, with their hands in fists,
pressing notebooks tight.

And schoolgirls, bearing in their satchels,
surely notes and diaries,
all of them in this alike:
blissful, Russian, and naïve.

And oh, world-wide decay, pass on and never
cut this tie of times—we need its aid.
For, certainly, two Russians cannot ever
exist or two Akhmatovas be made.

II

In another grave, not far away,
like a folk song by the Bible's side
a woman near Akhmatova in age
lay simply dressed, in white.

She lay as if awaiting a marriage
with nothing left to darn or wipe or sweep:
a peasant, said her face, her hands, her carriage,
a domestic, it would seem.

To be no more—how heavenly a state.
The people of the house were kind enough,
and like a child before a holiday
they washed and neatly dressed her up.

True, they didn't smother her with lilies,
but the coffin fit, and, oh,
such fancy slippers on her, new ones nearly
with the repairman's stamp still on the soles.

And there she lay, absolvingly serene,
her dry hands folded on her breast,
reverentially, it seemed,
as if they had a candle there to press.

Alive, those hands, (so skilled at this) had scurried
(writing, true, mere turns and twists)
dark and stern and strong as bronze
and never known a kiss.

Then I thought: perhaps, just suppose
two different Russias do exist:
a Russia of the hands and of the soul,
two different lands that never mixed.

No one ever mourned that woman. Night
dropped upon her with no dawn to come.
And above her, high, aloofly white
Akhmatova's patrician profile hung.

Akhmatova, above mere honor
reposed in state: disdainful, droll.
Acknowledging the high rank placed upon her
above the low impostures of the soul.

Aristocrat! Fair denizen, conveyed
on roadways ringing to the prancing trotters.
Yet her hands, afloat on a bouquet
seemed to rock and, rocking, seemed betrayed.

They labored to their limit, but at times
they reached beyond their strength, and then,
so light in Pushkin's hold, the pen
with sudden weight would grin and break her fingers.

Done with the swift chill of Aix wine
and kisses caught in Petersburg and Nice,
these fingers met upon her breast, resigned
and fragrant with a peasant girl's fatigue.

Without a staff, without a crown a queen
among the tarnished gifts of state and man,
she lay absolvingly serene,
like the woman dressed in secondhand.

And in that other grave the woman lay
who never looked on Nice, and on her brow
appeared Akhmatova's stern grace.
And between them there was no frontier.

TRANSLATED BY ANTHONY KAHN

IN JEST

Goodbye, fame! Put someone else in my niche.
I'd swap a seat in the President's jeep
for a warm corner in a ditch
where I could go soundly off to sleep.
Oh, how I would unload my fears,
pour all my deadly, dreary pride
into the burdocks' hairy ears
as I lay fidgeting on my side.
And I would wake up, with unshaven chin,
amongst the bugs and little insects.
Oh how marvelously unknown!—
someone fit to dance gypsy steps.
Far off, people would grasp for power,
hang by their nails from the top of the tower,
but none of this would send me sour,
in a ditch I would be lower.
And there, embracing a mangy dog,
I would lie down and make my berth
in the friendly dust, holding dialogue
on the highest level—of the earth.
Alongside, the bare feet of a girl
would float innocently by,
and pale blades of grass would twirl
down from the haycarts between me and the sky.

On a bench a smoker would toss out
a cigarette pack, squashed and empty,
and from the label the twisted mouth
of Blok would sadly smile at me.

TRANSLATED BY GEOFFREY DUTTON
WITH IGOR MEZHAKOFF-KORIAKIN

THE STAGE

The curse upon me,
the waste of my soul in rage,
is the stage . . .

I was young.
Wanted to climb a pedestal,
wanted the showers of applause and flowers
when I came forward
and stood, feeling laughable,
on the talcum powder left from the ballet shoes.
As yet I had absolutely nothing to say,
there was only this ringing inside me,
in my throat,
but something was trying so powerfully to come out
that no stage fright could frighten it away.
And as my breaking voice began to cry,
time, breaking itself, began to shout
and I was that moment of time,
and it was I.
And on the stage
in the fiery line of the footlights
it was as if all those things still unexpressed,
hiding their tiny glow within the darkness,
were suddenly in me and I was one great light.

The mystique of the stage was set in motion
and fame stood separate beside us, as the third.
As in the Bible,
in the beginning was the word,
and then—well then,
in the word was the explosion.
You fools—
of course I'm no great actor!
My bones had no strength in them yet, I know,
but on my face, hacking
away the pimples,
the features of Mayakovsky began to glow.
And the golden head of Sergey Yesenin,
of all poets the most reckless, the craziest,
with the scent of the wide wheatfields of his origin,
rose above my head, and I was possessed.
My teachers,
I have not disgraced you, I swear,
and secretly I have given my laurels back to you.
The whole world was applauding us together,
Paris and Melbourne,
and London,
and Hamburg.
But what have you done to me,
O stage—
is your hunger assuaged?
My verse did not soften
or disintegrate,
but became cruder and cruder
in style and theme.

Stage,
you gave me the light in which to scintillate
but took away the soft shadow and the subtle gleam.
I was turning purple from the intolerable strain.
I was painting great placards,
rationalizing slyly
that a watercolor can hardly be seen
in a large hall,
especially from the gallery.
I began to cherish not quietness—
but thunder,
and when you do this it is easy to go wrong.
I could throw the bright colors around,
make people wonder,
but forgot the intimate shades are just as strong.

And then there was something even more terrible:
when the audience were slipping into their coats
bits of me were scattered amongst thousands of people,
and I was leaving the hall myself,
becoming remote.
And my double,
pock-marked with perspiration,
would sit in the make-up room,
a finished magician,
thousand-faced
with all the accumulation
of other faces inside him,
beyond recognition.

O stage—

why pay such a horrible wage?

"Goodbye, stage . . ."—

I will whisper quietly,

although I have forgotten the art of whispering.

I will abandon noise and listen for a rustling,

leaning on the slender shoulder of a birch tree.

But, demanding my help, as the moment before the storm

demands the coming explosion

and the scatter of birds,

everything unexpressed in distant fields and farms

tightens in my throat

and fuses into words.

The degradation of the living and the dead,

in this world

still so far from paradise,

still demands my help,

dragging the shreds

of my voice from the chords I vulgarized.

I am not jealous, other poets are my friends.

I don't need anything—I'll give away all my reserves,

my throat,

yes, even my voice that so often offends,

in order that you may have what you deserve!

Of course, it will be quite obvious to posterity

That I—

alas!—

represent no ideal,

and yet
        whether crudely, or with some dexterity,
from the stage I did awaken some kind feelings.
And I will mutter hoarsely,
                                        when there is left
not even a whisper of my voice's pride:
"O stage,
        I was what I was, only myself,
and whether I lived as I should have—
                                                        let God decide."
And I will leave the stage for darkness with some courage,
O stage . . .

TRANSLATED BY GEOFFREY DUTTON
WITH IGOR MEZHAKOFF-KORIAKIN

IDOL

Down in the pine needles
in the snowstorm-stogged ravine
an Evenki idol stands
fixing his eyes on the *taiga*.

Aggressively squinting,
he watched until the time came
when Evenki women started
hauling presents to him.

They brought him mukluks and parkas,
they brought him honey and fur,
figuring that he'd pray
but mainly think for them all.

In the dark assurance
that he'd understand,
they'd smear his mouth
with warm deer blood.

But what could he do, the phony
little god,
with his fierce, wooden
whittled-down soul?

Now he's looking through the branches,
abandoned and dead.
No one believes in him;
no one prays to him.

Did I just dream this up? At night
in his ravine, far off yonder,
he sets his eyes
on fire, overgrown with moss,

And listening to the snowstorm
blast down, licks
his lips. Lord, I know it.
He wants blood.

TRANSLATED BY JAMES DICKEY
WITH ANTHONY KAHN

OLD BOOKKEEPER

I don't have any pain. None at all.
Really, I don't estimate anything
unnecessary. Cramming a pillow under the seat
of my pants, I sit down in black oversleeves.

Here the same signatures and stamps
are. On the table papers rustle,
rustle, tired out, and so sadly
rustle, saying I'll be sixty. Soon.

Ah, the Chief—he's young! Powerful!
Today like always, shaved just so . . .
Fiddling with rosaries made out of
paper clips, talking to me about football.

Ah, the Chief! . . . he's clean *enough,*
and not so *much* of a son-of-a-bitch,
but I can see everything he's trying to hide
under that slick shine, his face.

Ah, the Chief—How easy he is
on himself! He wears those signet rings!
Only he don't walk so straight
in his beautiful new suede shoes!

I'll leave this little office. I'll smile,
not knowing why, at spring,
and get on the train that goes out
to Mytischchi, and everywhere farther away.

I'll get off where four ugly women
Live by the river. They're old, too.
One of them's gotten so tired that
any day I'll ask her to marry me.

And when I go back to my closet
in stillness that reminds me of "Prima,"
from the big wormy chest of drawers
I'll take out one snapshot.

There, hands propped on clumsy hipbones,
looking straight into History
at its worst, I stand, a civil guardsman,
not young, in the great year '41.

I'll hear the rumble of planes,
shots and wild songs in the wind,
and my lips will whisper something,
but I can't make it out, myself.

1958

TRANSLATED BY JAMES DICKEY
WITH ANTHONY KAHN

SECRET MYSTERIES

Adolescent mysteries melt away
like mist upon the shore
The Tonyas and Tanyas were all mysteries
even with cold sores on their legs

Stars and animals were mysteries
Mushrooms under aspen trees
and doors creaking mysteriously—
only in childhood do doors creak that way

The world's riddles rose up
like balloons from the mouth
of some seductive fakir
full of crafty schemes

Enchanted snowflakes
fell in fields and woods
Enchanted laughter
danced in young girls' eyes

Mysteriously we whispered something
on the mysterious ice of a skating rink
mystery touching mystery
hand touching hand

Unexpectedly maturity caught up with us
His dress coat worn to holes
the fakir went on tour
in someone else's childhood

We grown-ups forgotten
Ah, fakir, you're a faker!
So unmysterious it hurts
snow falls on our shoulders

Where are you, bewitched balloons?
There's no mystery to our mourning
Others are unmysterious to us
and we're unmysterious to them

And if some hand by chance
caress us lightly
it still is only a hand and not a mystery
a hand, understand, only a hand

Oh give me a mystery, some simple mystery
a secret mystery—silence and timidity—
a fragile mystery, a barefoot mystery—
just one sweet secret mystery!

1960

TRANSLATED BY LAWRENCE FERLINGHETTI
WITH ANTHONY KAHN

□ □ □

A girl was playing the accordion;
the tide of wine was in her head,
and garlic made the blunt end glisten
on a loaf of bread.

It took no breach of blood or brass
to raise a banquet in a shack.
Geologists in arms we were
who caught her song and sang it back.

I knew a girl who knew the land;
I sat beneath her steady chair
and heard her unfamiliar hand
ride my rustling hair.

I sort of drank, I sort of didn't,
and mined the levels of my pain;
I sort of wasn't her beloved
and her beloved all the same.

The other girl did push and pull
a sigh of seas and distant shores
and sang it to the lap of rubber
boots that rubbed her legs and sores.

She sang of lonely, burning days,
an ache at heart, an ash of grief,
of limitless and faraway
fences, fires, trees.

The girl sang on and always on;
her sister, schooled in dust and stone,
wept until the quiet dawn
the tears of old, forgotten bones.

1955

TRANSLATED BY ANTHONY KAHN

THE MARK OF CAIN

In Memoriam R. Kennedy

The poor pilgrims dragged themselves wearily
along to Mecca through gray Syria,
huddled
          and doubled up
the pilgrims stumbled along—
away from delusion and ferment
to repent,
               repent,
                         repent . . .
And I was standing like an impenitent sinner
On the summit of the mountain
where once upon a time
                                   (don't stir!)
Abel was killed by Cain.
And—of all communiques of blood
               the most unforgettable—
the elemental voice was heard:
"Cain,
        where is your brother Abel?"
But once again the Pharisees,
the fascists
               with their vile-sweet voices:

"Why do you worry about visions that are fake?
Yes,
    with Abel maybe we should have held back.
Admittedly, there was a little mistake,
But generally speaking we were on the right track . . ."
And I was standing on the summit
between those ahead and the hosts behind,
above a world
                where people could commit
every corruption of their own kind.
There was no lightning
                and no thunder,
but the stones were crying with mouths opened wide:
"The corruption of the soul may be bloodless
but it is also fratricide!"
And I imagined a gloomy, dead
brick orphanage,
                where as with henbane
the children of Abel are spoonfed
with lies by the children of Cain.
And in the faces of Abel's children,
doing what they know that they must do,
which is always to stay silent,
the red mark of Cain shows through . . .

And I, no one's murderer,
was standing
                on the sticky summit,
but my conscience murmured
like the Bible:

"You won't be able to quit!
You're corrupting your spirit with lies,
and your spirit is crumbling,
cracking inside.
And to kill yourself
—you cannot disguise
that that is also fratricide!
And how many women, you twister,
lie like crucifixions along your way—
but women, they are your sisters,
worth more than brothers can repay.
And the Hussars' toasts 'To the Ladies,'
what are they worth?
Bravado,
snide.
To kill love—
you cannot evade it,
that is also fratricide.
And someone's gray
brown eyes
staring at you with disdain,
on your forehead cicatrize
you with the eternal mark of Cain . . ."
I shuddered:
—Quiet, O conscience.
You know this is not comparable,
it is like comparing a children's circus
with a bloody Roman shambles . . .
But the shadow of bony Cain
jutted out from the rocks near at hand,

and the blood of the brother he had slain
was endlessly dripping from my hand.
"Look—
          my bloody hands shake.
As a child it was fun to improvise,
out of curiosity to break
the velvet wings of butterflies.
Everything begins with the butterflies
and then—
          fratricide!
What will you say
                    to the eternal skies
and the court of stars
                         when you cannot turn back—
To say I am sinless would be telling lies,
but generally speaking I'm on the right track!
You know, all those whom you hate
set this up as the true state,
while the cigarettes take on
the smell of burning flesh, the Winstons
                                        and the Kents,
and the bullet
               which passed through John
kills Robert Kennedy.
And the bombs charge the earth, turn
brown villages blood-red, fire-black.
Admittedly they fall on children,
but generally speaking they're on the right track . . .
Everything begins with the butterflies,
later it comes round to bombs . . .

No amount of washing purifies—
the blood on your hands will be your doom.
The only murder which is fit—
is to kill
the Cain inside!"
And I losing my footing on the sticky summit
face to face with the infinite
tore the flesh open in my side
and the strangled
embryo Cain
died.
I was strangling everything mean and evil,
all that later you would despise,
but it was far too late to heal
the broken wings of the butterflies.
And the wind, blood-soaked, invisible,
lashed at me from the fury of space
as if the pages of the Bible
were lashing
me
on my face.

Damascus-Moscow
1967–1968

TRANSLATED BY GEOFFREY DUTTON
WITH IGOR MEZHAKOFF-KORIAKIN

KAMIKAZE

And I shudder
and come to my senses—Look!
His elbows dug into the green table,
a former kamikaze pilot—a dead man, Japanese,
truly—is talking about Raskolnikov.
At a "Symposium on the Novel," he's forty-five,
an old man. He's like
polite sobbing . . .
he's like a scream
strangled by a necktie. And through us
and somewhere past us,
through Shimonoze flak and the shade of Lazo,
like the yellow shine of Hiroshima,
reeling,
his face flies past.
But in his throat you can't tell
whether it's a lump of tears
or a cough-lump, or what.
The Emperor wanted him to grow
up
humble, his death already assigned . . .
a kamikaze.

Sure, it's great to swim along
hands and bouquets, to be slapped on the back by the military
there, at the parade. Sure,
it's fine to be a "hero of the people." But hero
in the name of *what?*
With a few buddies,
this one shucked off his hero-status
and said he'd just as soon stay
alive.
That took more guts than exploding
for a god-damned lie!
I'm supposed to be hell-for-leather
myself,
but what of my life and death, really?
What *do* I think, sinful and mortal,
among sinful, mortal people?
We're all assigned our deaths . . .
We're kamikazes. The "divine wind" . . .
the wind of death whistles in our ears:
every footfall on this bomb-cratered planet
is a step toward death.
So what if I get busted-up and crushed
but not because a dictator says so? I'll pull the control column
up by the roots
firewall the throttle
on collision course, and go out
like the last battering ram.

But sons, daughters,
descendants,
though my body sifts down in ashes, I'd like,
from the scraps of my plane, something good to explode
through to you.
How strange it is, though,
to seem to yourself always dying
in the sky for not
anything! To turn out to be lied-to
And still living in the face of your death-
assignment, and to be evil
as well! Yes, a living evil
long since supposed to be gone!

TRANSLATED BY JAMES DICKEY
WITH ANTHONY KAHN

AN ATTEMPT AT BLASPHEMY

Turning to the eternal magnet
in the pitch-dark night of my soul
I whisper my only prayer:
"O Lord, forgive me, help me."

And the Lord forgives and helps,
however helplessly he shrugs
at man's prolonged ingratitude
for his many mercies.

Clearly his people frighten God.
Call him by any name you choose—
Jehovah, Buddha, Allah—
he's one, and tired of being God.

If he could dematerialize,
or shrink in scale to a pocket idol,
he'd gladly slip away and hide
from our slobber in a private corner.

But it's not right for him to hide,
or stoop, like an African slave.
God also wants to believe in god,
but there's no god in the world for God.

And when, neglectful of our obligations,
we stick him with rotten little petitions,
to whom shall he address his prayer,
"O Lord, forgive me, help me"?

TRANSLATED BY STANLEY KUNITZ
WITH ANTHONY KAHN

AT THE MILITARY REGISTRATION AND ENLISTMENT CENTER

To the low cradle-song of the rails,
like a bone-tired oiler of expresses,
Zima Station slept on and on.
And the steeple on the District Soviet slept,
and a drunk slept in the cunette
and the watchman by the Grain Storage Center.

Like a Zima man, no Muscovite,
I walked and walked, breathing the smoke from my tobacco,
through the rustle of leaves and through somebody's dreams.
The rain touched the snare of the tin roofs . . .
And suddenly I heard a woman:
"Ah, if only there wasn't a war."

The moon slipped through piles of straw,
through little porches, shutters, slatted fences,
and, stopped right in my latest tracks,
sensing something of the future, I saw—
beheld, maybe—like a sad shade of the night,
a woman: one.

She was listening to something hidden in everything
that was dozing off. Her age; well, she was getting on
with it: fifty, at least; maybe more.
She was running along the handrails
with her palm, in a special way, a widow's way,
under the weathered-out signboard on the building:
"The Zima Military Registration and Enlistment Office."
Most likely she was coming from work
when something overran her, pushed her like a wave
to those handrails . . . in her the war came back
to life:
        a war without flags, without bands,
a war that had taken her breadwinner.
                                        And here,
leaning on the handrails
—the same ones, the same as before—
she sent a prayer down the tracks after her husband,
and then walked on, heavy with child
and with a right hand whose strength had gone
touched you, handrails, again, and in her left
like death, she held
a Notice: the Notice of all
Notices.
        Ah, if only there wasn't a war!
(His hands held an accordion)
        If only there wasn't . . .
(and a spoon stuck in his right boot)
        . . . a war, if only there wasn't . . .
(a crumb of tobacco on his lip)
        . . . a war . . .

(He was loud when he was drunk a little,—
"Now don't you worry about Leshka!
Not a damn thing's going to happen."—
but in his eyes, a deep pain,
looking out.)
Ah, if only there wasn't a war!

TRANSLATED BY JAMES DICKEY
WITH ANTHONY KAHN

HURRY IS THE CURSE OF OUR CENTURY

Hurry is the curse of our century
and man, mopping the sweat from his forehead,
zigzags through life like a pawn in a fury
of being trapped on the board with his time expired.

Hurriedly we drink, hurriedly we love,
our souls eroding go to waste.
Hurriedly we push and shove
and later we repent, at haste.

But at least once, whether your home
in the world is sleeping or boiling with untruths,
stop, like a horse smothered in foam
sensing the abyss before its hooves.

For God's sake stop, even half way,
trust Heaven, as you would your fate,
think—even if you do not pray
to God—at least of your own state.

When the collapsing leaves flutter,
when the locomotive gives its hoarse cry,
know this: the tired runner is pitiful,
the one who has stopped stands high.

Sweep off the dust of vanity of vanities,
at last remember eternity,
and holy indecision will freeze
your feet to immobility.

There is strength in indecision
when you hesitate to follow
the path leading to perdition
at the end of which false beacons glow.

As you trample on people's faces like leaves,
stop! Like Vij,* you are blind.
Don't forego this last reprieve
by rushing on with a mad wind.

When you stride so confidently towards your goal
over bodies as though they were steps,
stop—you who have forgotten God—
you are really stepping on yourself!

When spite is shoving you forward,
making your own soul a hypocrite,
towards the disgrace of a shot or a word—
don't hurry, don't do it!

* Vij is a blind monster-gnome of Ukrainian folklore whose eyelids touch the ground; if his eyes are opened nothing can be hidden from them. "Vij" is also the title of Gogol's romantic story with a Ukrainian setting of witchcraft.

Stop, O people of the Earth as you run
so blindly to the next assault!
Bullet, freeze as you fly from the gun,
and you, bomb in mid-air, halt!

O man, whose very name is sacred,
lifting the prayer of your eyes like a periscope
over disintegration and hatred,
for God's sake stop, for God's sake stop!

1968

TRANSLATED BY GEOFFREY DUTTON
WITH IGOR MEZHAKOFF-KORIAKIN

IV
Procession
with the Madonna

THE CONFESSIONAL

The little window of the confessional . . .
approaching it, in the religious shade
the threadbare face of a ravaged woman,
flickering with hope.

A child of the purlieus of Naples
waits her turn at the side,
an open Bible
on her telltale belly.

Without rifle or service cap
a soldier comes to be judged,
the skin of his back twitching
under the coarse uniform.

Housewives lug from the washtubs
and gamblers from the races
the sins of their imagination
along with their real sins.

Is there no confessional for me?
To whom shall I go, quelling my fears,
with the sinful dust, the foreign dust,
on my errant feet?

Enough of idleness and sloth!
What's the address? I'll find the way.
But people are crawling in my path,
begging to confess to me.

How can the confessor teach
those who are lost and sick at heart,
when he himself, among the sinners,
is worst, and most forsaken?

It is only a game we play
with other people's sins.
Besides, everyone knows
that everyone lies confessing.

And the priest lies too,
wanting to be good to them;
for the cozy fib, the double fib,
coddles and does not burn.

But I have no right to have faith in faith,
however I smash my brains on the stones,
when, almost like a truth to a truth,
a lie confesses to a lie.

Naples-Moscow

TRANSLATED BY STANLEY KUNITZ
WITH ANTHONY KAHN

THE HEAT IN ROME

Monks,
all soutanes left to the devil,
Dive into those Roman fountains!
All right,
Signor premier-ministro,
Into the Po with you! Right down,
Presto-presto! *You!* Get on down
Under it!
And like burros
and like mules
To the water, ambassadors!
To the water, ambassadors' wives!
Millionaire,
holler in sheer confusion,
"Mister, can you spare me some shade?"
Get together for once—
big shots
With the simple people!
O you common sweat!
*Every*thing's sweat-soaked—
feelings too.
Newspapers are sticky underwear:

The Madonna cries . . .
A miracle!
Miracle!
But don't you believe it—
sweat's pouring off her.
Over forty Centigrade . . .
the thermometer explodes;
Mercury dances dead-drunk in the dust
Like little world-globes
That the countries have all slipped off.
Everything melts to pieces, ravels—
Everything's gotten so soft—
even the State.
Gouge off
the temple-marble
And munch it like chewing gum.
And the bronze-coated kings,
heroes,
gods
are as miserable as
They'll ever be, as if made of plasticine:
Poke 'em with your finger;
they'll fall down.
On the Piazza dell' Indipendenza
I drown, more helpless than a baby,
up to my chest
In melted asphalt.
Hey! Anybody!
ANYbody!

No, damn it—
Nobody answers.
Living independently . . . ?
You could call it
Drowning independently!
And over it all
A bare-ass poet drones out
prophetic lines:
"The cows in the pastures've all rotted,
The Milky Way has curdled in the sky,
Peoples and vegetables give off all
Kinds of stinks! Awful currents of air!
SALVATION! It's in peeling off! A mass striptease!
Friends!
Romans!
Don't turn yourselves into corpses!
Don't be afraid of beauty! It's *virginal!*
Only cop-outs wear clothes!
Rip off your jockey shorts! Your
panties!"
Ladies gasp, "I've *got* to have it! OZONE! Some *Ozone,* for God's
sake!"
They've announced,
giving wings to the tailors,
that the fashionable thing to wear *this* season
Is the dress of the naked king.
"Ha HA! All History tells you
It's been the *real* fashion
for *thousands* of years!"

"O dear deputy of ours, you never take one step
into the villages,
but the villages have gotten gut-poor . . .
Where is everything you promised?"
"I promised?
Ah yes! Ah yes indeed!—
I forgot . . . but you'll forgive me! It's just this *heat!"*
"Why're you so limp, Baby?
Can we straighten you out with
wine?
Let's lie in the ice-box . . .
maybe things'll work out in
there . . ."
Deputies before their constituents
impotents before their wives
Killers before prosecutors
lawyers before killers
All justify themselves, good-naturedly as anything:
"There's no *air!* It's stuffy!
Stuffy, and hot from lies. RUSSIA!
Lend us some of that damned
SNOW!" But rumors're all over—pure gibberish!—that there's no
snow
In Russia!
And new rumors
Are flying
circling Rome
That there are no icebergs
At the Poles
that books are turning green

With mold in the libraries
that in the museums the colors are
dripping
From the pictures.
And the weakening City of Night doesn't
sleep.
You've got to decide something
Right *now!* Make up your mind, even if those who never drew
breath
Say, "There's no air to breathe."
Lord! From the skin of the
world—
Dirty grease!
If only somebody could *ventilate*
The earth! All planes
missiles
destroyers
All submachine guns
rifles
and, with 'em,
The false coin of the orator's tongue
the bronze brows of heads
Of state who've lost out . . . melt 'em! MELT 'em!
Melt 'em
To make fans!
Fans! Ah, fans!
Fans.
Maybe it'd help *some* . . .

TRANSLATED BY JAMES DICKEY
WITH ANTHONY KAHN

RHYTHMS OF ROME

Get up!
Rome-the-giant-alarm-clock shrills by your head.
Whip up with a shaving brush the kissing foam.
And go out towards Rome!
Give yourself up to the dawn thud of shoes, hammers,
and the cries
of milkmaids, news vendors, bakers, green-grocers.
The nuns
with their starched white wings crackling trip in Indian file.
The coppers
in their clay mugs clatter appealing to passersby.
The prostitutes,
after their morning medical, go straight to pray in church.
In a café
the pot-bellied discuss the best cure for constipation.
Gypsy girls
jingle their coin-necklaces near an exhibit of "Super-Pop-Art."
Ministers
speed by in Mercedes. Their hands are calloused from playing
cards.
Hands
calloused from work drift on, expecting nothing.
Lemons
and men, in Italy, cost cheaper than anything else.

Where are
you hurrying, all of you people? Where are you crawling,
the boa constrictors
of the fire pumps, where water swirls strongly like sinews?
To Rome—all of you,
as though to a church for absolution,
and to a market-place,
where they may buy or sell you, perhaps.
I'd snatch
at what Rome has to offer, so as not to perish later in life.
I'd steal
a bit of its rhythm, but no! there's no snatching or stealing it.

There are many Romes,
but as a physical entity Rome hardly exists.
There are many rhythms—
no common rhythm, and that's the secret of its streets.
But I'll become
a bone-and rag man crying the torn tatters of Rome.
I shall swell
like a sponge sucking Rome into my pores.
Till night
I shall eavesdrop, and then sleep not a wink through the night,
an informant
to all mankind about you, Rome, and about myself.
Inside my shirt
I shall hide all that your alleys will shout,
will weep,
whisper, whistle, clang, and murmur.
Let my pursuit

of Rome, through Rome, break and fracture my bones—
like a tape
I shall eagerly wind Rome around me . . .

"Fire! Fire!
Signora Silvia's aflame!"
"But no,
you fool,
it's her apartment . . ."
"Search in the wardrobe—
you'll find personal linen
and that colander—
chuck them out of the window!
Throw down the divan
and the lid of the toilet bowl!
. . . and all's in a heap,
might as well bang your head on a
wall . . .
Stop,
you blockhead.
Where's our vase?
And where's
the album,
the family album? . . ."
"Shut up,
wife,
squealing won't help . . ."
". . . Why did I ever get married
after sinning?"
"Here,
take this rope,
and lower the TV set . . ."

"The damn thing is being lowered at last!"
"Don't cry,
    these are just
        saucepans and cans.
Come to,
    wife,
        look—you're all covered with
            down . . ."
"Let go,
    don't push.
        Wait, where's the Madonna?
The Madonna's
        burning!
            They left her upstairs!"
"Good grief,
    what a calamity.
        Did you hear that, my son?"
"Now they'll be locked out of paradise, neighbor.
It's eternal damnation—for Signora Silvia . . .
No Madonna . . .
They forgot her . . . Ai-ai-ai!"

"Who wants the Duce, who wants the Duce!
A fine portrait that!
Come, people,
    flock together,
        crowd round—
no better man in all the world!
The painter's brush—
            admittedly!—
is not that of a Matisse,
but there was a time when the Duce

used to please you *multissimo.*
Drift up,
  flea market,
and do your smart trading.
Among so many odd bird-and-fish,
this little bird is quite unique!
This day there are
no open bidders for the Duce,
but enough concealed ones:
I can tell them by their eyes.
It would serve them better to be bolder,
for the Duce is already cracking.
Who wants the Duce, who wants the Duce?
No one needs the Duce?"

"Come over here, Signore—we sell letters here.
Real letters—do you see the postmarks?
We request you not to remove the stamps—
  you can read the letters, don't hurry . . .
There are enough letters for all—piles of them.
Here is the eighteenth century, if you please:
  'I shall wait for you eternally.'
Here, if you please, is the nineteenth:
  'I shall wait for you a hundred years.'
And here's the twentieth, Signore:
  'Why do you keep twisting and turning?
I've already spent two evenings with you, and nothing doing.'
Here's a World War I letter,
  and one of World War II . . .
(Unfortunately, time has not restored the censor's deletions . . .)
And if there's a World War III, Signore, I imagine,
as you do, we'll be left with no letters at all.

Signore, I believe letters to be the most precious of relics,
but they are sold cheap, and I, old man, buy them.
Letters are the odd pages of a great book, perhaps,
but there's no glue to paste them all together."
"Don't you find it strange, Signor, to trade in letters?"
"Strange? What's strange about it?
    Aha, you must be a poet, I guess . . .
And don't you find it strange to trade in songs?
The world's full of strange things,
    but nothing is really strange . . ."

"Mama Roma, mama Roma,
don't you have a conscience?
My husband's as thin as a spaghetti,
a spaghetti without any sauce.
Conscience does not prick me—
all that pricks is my frisky blood.
Government,
    give us
        divorce laws,
or—
    I shall emigrate!"

"Signor doctor, please explain what sort of animal I am?"
"I don't understand your question, Signora."
"What's there not to understand, Signor doctor!
Soon as I rise I start darning, ironing, cooking
breakfast for my husband and children—
    just like a squirrel in a treadmill.
I don't have time to eat—I'm famished as a wolf.
I go to the factory and do the donkey work.
I return by bus and hiss spite like an old goose.

I go shopping and stagger back as loaded as a camel.
Back home, I launder again, sweep up and cook, work like a horse.
Dog-weary, I fall into bed.
My husband comes in drunk, plunks down,
and says: 'Make room, you old cow.'
What sort of an animal am I, Signor doctor, tell me that?"

"I'm at the end of my confession,
Padre.
I've no thick hair left, wisps are all
I have.
You taught us, Father, not to sin
but think.
Foolish me, I've tried, Padre, to live
like that.
As if it were a dream, I remember nothing.
In vain
I lived so righteously, it gives me
the creeps.
I'd like to sin before I die, but it's
too late.
I only remember the sins of very long
ago.
I have no need of anything now—being
a grandma.
It's a long way to the schooldays when I
wore a bow.
Come nearer, grandchildren, I've something
to tell you.
Like a small cross, in your hands I shall
place the truth.

My little ones, of necessary sins be not
afraid;
have fear, instead, of those tedious
coffins.
Run further away from a faith that is
empty
into sins, as into dense forest, a willow-branch
forest.
Quietly, there, grandchildren, amid moaning,
you'll hear:
your one joy before dying is to remember
your sins . . ."

"Lucky lottery tickets,
 tickets,
 tickets!
They'll give you motorbikes,
 Fiats,
 sideboards.
Don't believe in politics,
 or in fool-cybernetics,
believe only in lottery tickets,
 lucky tickets . . .
You wear birettas now,
 but tomorrow you'll be mere skeletons.
Snap up the tickets,
 the lucky tickets!"
"If failure's turned you bald,
 then don't be such dullards, Signori,
buy a policeman out-of-the-ordinary,
 a rubber one.

Pummel him,
    spit on him,
        kick him,
            shove him,
and when you teach him a thing or two,
then you'll get at least partial relief
    from the damnable life you lead . . ."
"And tell me, please
    won't you also have
ministers all made
    of rubber?"
"I won't even promise them.
I regret, Signor—
    they're all sold out."

"Hands off,
    hands off
        Vietnam!
Let's stop laundering now, daughter,
I'm a mother, that's certain.
Why are they bombing
those children—
    the little Vietnamese?
If they're not all childless,
then the papers must be lying."

"I don't give a damn for Vietnam!
I'm all for a quiet life.
All
    I need is a new patch
on my trousers!"

"Signor sergeant,
    Signor sergeant,
off the Piazza di Spagna
I was trying to buy a sideboard
and a secretary for the bedroom.
And suddenly in a gallery window I saw a bed,
and on the bed a girl,
wearing not a stitch as the day she was born,
puffing insolently on a cigarette.
And beside the girl lay
a pair of soiled panties,
and, in addition,
    Signor sergeant,
they were empty . . .
    those things.
And over this disgraceful show
was written:
    'Sculpture.'
Signor sergeant,
    save Rome
and Roman culture!"
"To save Rome, Signora, is complicated . . .
What's to be done . . .
    The younger generation . . .
One can't make out these days
what you can do or can't . . ."

"Striptease, in reverse,
    is the latest thing with us."
"What sort of thing is that?"
    "This is the way it works:

Out comes a floozy—
    wearing only pasties,
and then she starts dressing,
    and that's where the kick comes in."
"An old trick . . .
    all crawl out naked
        on the stage of life,
and then clothe themselves
    in words,
        words,
            words,
but, all the same, behind the words
    they see each other naked.
Striptease, in reverse—such is *la vita* . . ."

"Signor, it's none of my business, of course, but as the bar proprietor, I'd like to warn you about that woman, who has just sat down at your table. She is—if you'll excuse me, a man . . ."

"You're joking!"

"It's no joke. It's true to life, I regret, Signor. Observe the hands and legs—they are rather large and muscular. A special cream has been used to remove the facial hair. The long hair is either a wig or naturally grown. You may have been deluded by the rounded forms of the breasts? That is the result of paraffin injections. Painful, but effective. Signor, you are still very young and evidently inexperienced. Therefore I considered it my duty to warn you somewhat tactlessly . . ."

"You mean this woman is a man?"

"A man, Signor . . ."

"The devil! Incidentally, call me Signora, not Signor. For many days now I have been trying to find at least one genuine woman . . . But I've had no luck . . ."

"Signori!

In the name and at the instigation of the presidium of the Pederast Club allow me to propose the first toast to women. Let this toast be no surprise to you, Signori. For all their physical and moral deficiencies women are indispensable; they give birth to us, pederasts. So—here's to women!"

"Tell me, my friend, why should we write verses
amid this terrible disintegration? I don't know.
Though harshly you may try to make this world ashamed,
it refuses to be shamed. Like the flag, shame's been betrayed.

"Salvation lies in feeling ashamed, but that's forgotten,
and at times I have the urge to cry:
'O where, mankind, is your sense of shame—
which is your one and only powerful lever?'

"Shamelessness reigns about us in the night,
while feelings are diminished and maimed—
only the veined noses of the drunkards
blush red with shame for all mankind . . .

"Stop now, stop . . . Your bitter monologue
is verse already . . . It's worth writing verse then.
And if you're reluctant, God will compel you—
the God that groans in us, imperfect ones.

"Yes, shame's forgotten or, rather, it's quiescent,
but why break your heart on that account.
You still feel shame! Why have the others lost
their innate capacity for shame?

"Inactively to watch corruption
is no better than to be openly corrupt,
and, damning corruption from on high,
we ourselves become part of the corruption.

"And doesn't it seem to you, my friend,
that, because we've lost our sight through fear,
we find ourselves in a vicious circle,
unable to see the world beyond the line enclosing us?

"But there are different circles. There are
at this moment, too—intact, as of old—
love, hope, goodness, and honor,
all walking through Rome, unseen.

"They pass in the shade, and thus they see us, too.
They walk along. Like specters we are chased.
And it is they, perhaps, who are right
and eternal, just as this city is eternal.

"My love, we've been forgotten here.
From the park all the people have gone home,
and, leaving the ferris wheel,
the others have wandered off elsewhere.

"The operator was evidently well-meaning—
he did not drop us down to earth.
The great wheel has stopped.
We've been forgotten . . . That's very good!

"Below us lies our poor, proud Rome,
our beloved Rome, our accursed Rome.
It's not aware that we are hovering
in our cabin in the air above.

"Below us the lie-mongering politicians,
the ministers, the trollops, kings,
high personages, the police, the armed forces—
how utterly tedious all this is!

"Someone needs us there below,
and we have to do something about it.
So let's be thankful they've forgotten us
for a while up here in the sky.

"Give that cabin of ours a push
and put your lips to mine,
or I myself will push our cabin
and put my lips to thine."

Stop, war, stop, war . . .
Yes, like Rome, life is terrifying,
but, like Rome, there's only one life . . .
Stop, war, stop, war . . .

1965

TRANSLATED BY GEORGE REAVEY

PROCESSION WITH THE MADONNA

to Ludovico Corrao

I

In the small, untroubled town of Taormina
A grave procession passed with its Madonna.
Smoke from the candles rose and came to nothing,
As frail as any moment's brief enigma.

There in the forefront, all attired in white,
The young girls walked, holding their candles tightly.
Flushed with a timid rapture, on they came,
Full of themselves and of the world's delight.

And the girls stared at the candles in their hands,
And in those flames, unstable in the wind,
They saw stupendous meetings, deep communions,
And heard endearments past all understanding.

Oh, it was right that the young girls should be hopeful.
The hour of their deception was not ripe.
But there behind them, like their fates impending,
The women marched along with weary step.

Attired in black, the women marched along,
And they too held their candles tightly, strongly,

Heavily shuffling, grave and undeceived,
And full of an accustomed sense of wrong.

And the women stared at the candles in their hands,
And in those flames, unstable in the wind,
They saw the scrawny shoulders of their children
And heard the vacant speeches of their husbands.

Thus, street by street, they all went on together,
Declaring that the Madonna was their mother,
And bearing the Madonna like some strange
Victim who stands erect upon her stretcher.

The Madonna's heart, or so it appeared, was pained
Both for the girls and for the women behind them;
And yet—or so it appeared—she had decreed
That life go on like this, world without end.

I walked beside the Madonna, and my glance
Found in the candles no glad radiance,
No weary sorrow, but a muddled vision
Full of sweet hope and bitterness at once.

And so I live—still dreaming, still unmarried,
And yet already doomed forevermore—
Somewhere between the girls in their white dresses
And the grey women in their black attire.

Sicily

TRANSLATED BY RICHARD WILBUR
WITH ANTHONY KAHN

NEAR THE FORGOTTEN ROMAN ROAD

Near the forgotten Roman Road
not far away from Damascus,
the contours of the mountainsides erode
deathly as the Emperors' death masks.

Warming their scales, their heads withdrawn
into their coils, secret and obsessed,
fat snakes are basking in the sun—
just gone from Cleopatra's breast.

The road carried rubies and pearls
and swords of damascene, most rare
of steels, and the squirming slave girls
used to sweep it with their hair.

Pocked with the ulcers of Venus
their coats of mail never showed,
with faces like coins the legionaries
marched along the dead-straight road.

Not yet broken up for junk,
the swaying chariots leaned over
like the curved combs bent
through the Empress's coiffure.

The flagstones of the road were packed
tight by slaves bent with the load,
like their petrified backs
driven down into the road.

Quite exhausted by this fiery land
and the effort of thinking, a soft patrician,
a cup of lemon juice by his hand,
anointed himself with Etruscan lotion:

"Even if only the skulls and ribs
of this rabble are left under the sky,
we at least will not die like pigs
and the road itself will never die . . ."

And the Arab laborer obediently
cracking stones, yet a crafty slave,
a perfidious slave, was thinking obstinately
with every blow his sledgehammer gave:

"Flesh and blood you glorify,
but you have forgotten God.
All right then, even you will die,
all right then, so will the road . . ."

The roots of the empire were rotting in filth.
It was tatty with decrepitude
like an old patchwork quilt
sewn together with threads of blood.

They used the tortures they understood
and subtler pressures on the head,
they tried to mend it all with blood,
but there is no weaker thread.

Roman hypocrisy is naked
since the arrogant toga fell,
and the great empire is quite dead
and the road is dead as well.

They tried the forger's falsehood
that repeats, it has nothing to do with the road,
the road is not guilty of the blood,
the stones do not know why it flowed.

But the wild weeds have many times
well and truly settled the score.
The road which gave birth to crimes
is criminal itself for evermore.

And let all roads that run to hangmen
and all roads that run to tyrants' misdeeds
be rewarded by the highest payment,
which is the highest growth of weeds!

And these were my thoughts beside that road
now closed to soldier and chariot,
beside the road which forgot God
and which, for that reason, God forgot.

Damascus-Moscow
1967–1968

TRANSLATED BY GEOFFREY DUTTON
WITH IGOR MEZHAKOFF-KORIAKIN

V
Cemetery
of Whales

IN A STEELWORKER'S HOME

I love America,
  the America who swam
the Maytime Elbe
  holding aloft whiskey
with a tired right arm,
  paddling with the left;
yes, and Russia swam to meet her in
the Maytime Elbe,
  holding aloft vodka
with a tired left arm,
  paddling with the right,
and vodka and whiskey—
  neat!—without translation
understood
  each other perfectly,
    goddammit,
on the waters where victories met!

I love America,
  the America who now
sits with me in the prefab ranch-house
of a steelworker.

  On the worker's arms
blue veins bulge and fork,
like secret tributaries of our Elbe.
There are no governments between us now.
Our invisible government
  has been chosen by us wordlessly—
those same tired soldiers,
  boys from Irkutsk and Kentucky,
who invisibly swim to each other
  until today on the Maytime Elbe.

Murmuring, murmuring,
invisible waves surge
across the plain fraternal table,
and wineglasses of cheap Chianti,
cradled by us on these waves,
redden like guiding buoys.
We talk
  as if we were swimming
to embrace each other like brothers,
  BUT
for twenty years they have polluted the Elbe.
They've dumped so much sewage in her—
the backwaters of falsehood,
  our era's super-cesspools:
Newspapers soaked in poison,
  dregs of inflammatory speeches,
the spit of scoundrels,
  Kleenexes soggy with snot,
and greasy sweat fastidiously wiped

from the hypocrite faces of long-winded orators.
Beneath the surface of our Elbe are hiding
moss-covered mines of distrust
and sleek new submarines
pregnant with torpedoes,
offspring of a marriage of fear
  and science.

Oh, when
  will we understand each other
as vodka and whiskey—
  straight!—without translation
understood
  each other perfectly,
    goddammit,
on the waters where victory met victory!
Really, do we need a new Hitler
to unite us
  again?
A price
  like maybe
    much too high . . .
Russia and America,
  your path
to each other is tortuous,
  but I believe,
    do believe
that through all the refuse and the mossy mines,
  we will swim to one another,
    we will swim,

we will embrace
  as in the Maytime of '45,
and this time,
  I dare believe,
    for keeps!
True, there are oceans of malice between us.
True, the Great Ocean, the Pacific, is between us.
But we will swim it;
  no ocean so great
it cannot become an Elbe!

I love America,
  the America who now,
snuggled in her crib, wiggles her delicate toes;
her slender feet shine for us, the disenchanted,
like candles radiating hope.
What is her name—
  Jan?
    Or, perhaps, Lara?
Her eyes
  are huge
    and blue,
two trusting drops
of that same Elbe,
  our common Elbe
we must not betray.
Russia and America,
  swim closer!

TRANSLATED BY JOHN UPDIKE
WITH ALBERT C. TODD

MONOLOGUE OF A BROADWAY ACTRESS

Said an actress from Broadway
  time had pillaged like Troy:
"There are simply no more roles.
No role
  to extract from me all my tears,
no role
  to turn me inside out.
From this life, really,
  one must flee to the desert.
There are simply no roles any more!
Broadway blazes
like a hot computer
but, believe me, there's no role—
  not one role
amidst hundreds of parts.
Honestly, we are *drowning* in rolelessness . . .
  Where are the great writers! Where?

The poor classics have broken out in sweat,
  like a team of tumblers whose act is too long,
but what do they know
  about Hiroshima,
about the murder of the Six Million,
  about all our pain?!
Is it really *all* so inexpressible?
Not one role!
It's like being without a compass.
You know how dreadful the world is
when it builds up inside you,
  builds up and builds up,
and there's absolutely no way out for it.
Oh yes,
  there are road companies.
For that matter,
  there are TV serials.
But the *roles* have been removed.
They put you off with bit parts.
I drink. Oh I know it's weak of me,
but what can you *do,* when there are no more people,
no more roles?
Somewhere a worker is drinking,
  from a glass opaque with greasy fingerprints.
He has no role!
And a farmer is drinking,
  bellowing like a mule because he's impotent:
he has no role!

A sixteen-year old *child*
  is stabbed with a switchblade by his friends
    because they have *nothing* better to *do* . . .
There are no roles!
Without *some* sort of role, life
  is simply slow rot.
In the womb, we are all geniuses.
But potential geniuses become idiots
without a role to play.
Without demanding anyone's blood,
I
  do demand
    a *role!*"

1967

TRANSLATED BY JOHN UPDIKE
WITH ALBERT C. TODD

ON THE QUESTION OF FREEDOM

Dachau's ashes burn my feet
The asphalt smokes under me
Warheads & bayonets stuck
under my nails

I'll stroke a stray strand of my beloved's hair
And I myself shall smoke
crucified Christ-like on wings of bombers
flying through this night to kill Christ's kids

My skin trembles with explosions
as if it were Vietnam
and breaking my back and ribs
the Berlin Wall runs through me

You talk to me of freedom? Empty question
under umbrellas of bombs in the sky
It's a disgrace to be free of your own age
A hundred times more shameful than to be its slave

Yes I'm enslaved to Tashkent women
and to Dallas bullets and Peking slogans
and Vietnam widows and Russian women
with picks beside the tracks and kerchiefs over their eyes

Yes I'm not free of Pushkin and Blok
Not free of the State of Maryland and Zima Station
Not free of the Devil and God
Not free of earth's beauty and its shit

Yes I'm enslaved to a thirst for taking a wet-mop
to the heads of all the bickerers & butchers of the world
Yes I'm enslaved to the honor of busting the mugs
of all the bastards on earth

And maybe I'll be loved by the people for this
For spending my life
(not without precedent in this iron age)
glorifying unfreedom from
the true struggle for freedom

TRANSLATED BY LAWRENCE FERLINGHETTI
WITH ANTHONY KAHN

THE RESTAURANT FOR TWO

Honolulu,
you loll dreamily on your back in a silver-black nowhere.
The breeze moves moons
Across the waves and along your mermaidenly thighs.
ubiquitous scintillation.
Like a savage, you adore glinting trinkets in shopwindows.
Like brooches
great ships ride pinned in your watery hair.
In heedless brown hands
you shuffle Yanks, Japs, and cards from Down Under.
You dance,
and tiny gilded fish tinkle in your heels.
A Scots laird
in a multicolored kilt reels with you, drooling,
and lubriciously
slips his hand under somebody's skirt, not his own.
But a modest hut,
a "Restaurant à deux," on its pilings of palm
like a gnome on stilts
has attained to the stars, a unique toy temple.
No aërial
tops its conical cap of green leaves.

Within, the walls
are woven of bamboo and mystery, and what takes place
is *hush-hush.*
A "boy," Malayan, smirking, fetches up the stairway
baked shark's fin
steeped in pineapple, golden through and through.
Two places set.
Two candles. Two conspirators. Two fugitives.
Into each other's eyes
as if into cathedrals they have fled the world's bedlam.
It's shaky in here,
it's rickety as a Chinese lantern. Maybe it's wicked.
It's false, sure.
That is to say, it's substanceless—and still, so pleasant!
The samba's throb,
the stars' murmuring, the thunder from the breakwater—
all for these two.
Gladly I would beat it to that Restaurant à deux.
I would crush
my glass of flat champagne and shout to the sourpussed mob:
"I am dying,
you bore me so. I yearn for the Restaurant à deux."
Oh no, you say?
One must do this, do that, but never, never the other?
I am fed up.
I am tired to death. I want *in* to the Restaurant à deux.
Reconsider?
Struggle on, be committed? Oh, I gave it a whack—so what?
That little hut
has shown me the answer, the exit, the Restaurant à deux.

Let them judge me!
I'm off! And yet, running away . . . is cowardly stuff.
WHAT WOULD HAPPEN
IF EVERYBODY WERE TO HIDE IN A RESTAURANT À DEUX?!
That's no way out,
in an epoch of open wounds—to seek shelter from ennui
in a gnome-home,
in the tresses and lips of another, in her knees and brow.
A demon's whisper
impels us to flee; we cannot comprehend
that after flight
it is even worse than before to be a galley-slave.
. . . Amid the stars,
they sit as in a dainty boat, having had their fun, at peace,
two fugitives:
while below them, life with its dogs like a sheriff waits.
The Malayan
daydreams at the foot of the sacrosanct stairway
and scornfully
entertains a stir of pity for innocence so hollow.
He observes
a half-hour remains to closing time (then, scram!)
and switches on
the birdsong tape-recorded to lend the illusion of paradise.

1967

TRANSLATED BY JOHN UPDIKE
WITH EDWARD KEENAN

A BALLAD ABOUT NUGGETS

Night. The town of Fairbanks sleeps,
exhausted. But invisible
squeakings walk the snowy streets
cloaked in hides and wool.
Wearing the face of an adolescent
and a painted caribou parka,
an Eskimo strip-tease *artiste*
hurries to work in a bar.
Drunken fliers from the air base,
aching for a shack-up,
ruttish louts, brave buddies,
throw snowballs at her back.
But she in darkness carries
her frozen breath
through the leers like a pure
white rose in her teeth.
In out of the cold
as hoary as owls,
in through the saloon doors
come clamorous clouds
with people inside them!—
a miner, a hunter, a trapper.
They all toss their caps
on the walrus-tusk hatrack.

Who comes from where?
What nation? Who cares!
Among these Alaskans
I'm one of the bears;
for us holy vodka
will answer all prayers.
Pal Bob, fellow sourdough, have a drink,
down the hatch.
Your big mitts have hugged me,
your stiff whiskers scratch.
Your grin gleams with gold.
You look worn out, man.
"Listen, Rooshian, I've been prospecting
all my life, understand?
No ruddier bastard than me swung a pick.
Now I'm trash.
My bald head's a runway
for mosquitoes and gnats.
Now I'm set to cash in,
to add it up proper:
a mouthful of gold
and a fistful of copper.
Ah, when I buried my old lady, Viv,
I recall how the sled-dogs gave
a howl at the edge of the hole,
at the edge of her grave.
Viv was a knockout once, just like
those Playgirls you unfold.
Her body white as quartz all over,
with little flecks of gold.

I had a good eye then, as young as you,
as lucky and game.
I said to her: 'I've staked you out.
Viv, you're my claim.'
I tortured her for forty years.
I was crazy,
Lifelong crazy, to find my strike,
to find nuggets.
She didn't ask for fancy clothes
but, shyly,
for a son. She dreamt of a son like me,
and I, of nuggets.
I drank. Like yellow fish
alive in a muddy sea,
they came at me, teased me,
nuggets.
So I closed up shop,
a bankrupt boss.
My pick and shovel
made Viv a cross.
I ain't forgot how I dragged that box
on the hard-froze earth.
I never dug up my nugget,
I buried her."
Bob counts the coppers in his paw.
He is drunk, disconsolate.
"Without gold, I . . . 'Scuse me, Rooshian,
lend me a stake."
Having forgotten his cap,
he shakily seeks the way out

and jabs the swinging doors
and plunges into his cloud.
Then I too wander in the dark,
a child of the saloon.
Nothingness pulls on my pockets
as I walk along.
I still haven't shut up shop,
I'm too timid;
but perhaps my nugget
is already buried.
Boyfaced beside me,
a silent companion,
the Eskimo-stripper,
exhausted, hurries home.
Zero. Icicles
beard my chin,
and birds frozen in flight fall
like nuggets, with a clink.

1967

TRANSLATED BY JOHN UPDIKE
WITH EDWARD KEENAN

CEMETERY OF WHALES

A cemetery of whales:
  in a snowy graveyard
instead of crosses
  their own bones stand.
They couldn't be gnawed by teeth;
  teeth are too soft.
They couldn't be used for soup;
  pots are too shallow.
The straining wind bends them,
  but they keep their position,
rooted in ice,
  arching like black rainbows.
Thirsty for a snort,
  an Eskimo hunchback,
shaped like a question mark,
  huddles in them as in parentheses.
Who playfully clicked a camera?
  Restrain your photophilia.
Let's leave the whales in peace,
  if only after death.

They lived, these whales,
  without offense to people,
in infantile simplicity,
  reveling in their own fountains,
while the crimson ball of the sun
  danced in a torrent of rays . . .
Thar she blows!
  Come on, lads, let's get 'em!
Where can we hide?
  But you're broader than space!
The world doesn't hold enough water
  for you to dive under.
You think you're God?
  A risky bit of impudence.
One harpoon, smack in the flank,
  rewards enormity.
Enormity commands everyone
  to hunt for it.
Whoever is big is stupid.
  Who's smaller is wiser.
Sardines, like vermicelli,
  are an impossible target,
lost in the generic—
  but greatness is helpless.
On board, binoculars tremble
  as the crew takes aim;
streaming harpoon in his side,
  huge Tolstoy runs from the Kodak.

A baby whale, not full-fledged,
  though evaluated as a whale,
Esenin flutters and kicks,
  hoisted high on a harpoon shaft.
The title of Whale is a bloody dignity.
  Greatness kills greatness.
Mayakovsky himself
  pounds in the lance.
The shallows are also a menace:
  dashed on the shoals by the chase,
Gorky hawks and disgorges
  fragments of steel and hickory.
Without even moaning,
  gliding along the path of blood,
Pasternak with a snatch of lime
  sinks into Lethe.
Hemingway is silent;
  but from his grave a threatening shaft
shoots out of the grass,
  growing up from the coffin.
And hidden behind the mob,
  murder in his eye,
the Dallas whaler
  with a telescopic sight.
A big drive is on;
  we cherish their names posthumously.
Your law is more honest,
  cruel Alaska.

166

In the cemetery of whales
  by the hummocks of ice
there are no sanctimonious flowers:
  the Eskimos have tact.
Hey, Eskimo hunchback,
  white men have a funny custom:
after planting the harpoon,
  they weep over the corpse.
Murderers mourn like maidens,
  and tearfully suck tranquilizers,
and parade in crêpe,
  and stand honor guard.
The professional hunters,
  who would look out of place,
send wreaths to the whales
  from the State Bureau of Harpoonery.
But the flowers are twisted together
  with steel cables and barbs.
Enough of such goodness!
  Let me live among Eskimos!

1967

TRANSLATED BY JOHN UPDIKE
WITH ALBERT C. TODD

NEW YORK ELEGY

At night, in New York's Central Park,
chilled to the bone and belonging to no one,
I talked quietly with America:
both of us were weary of speeches.

I talked with my footsteps—
unlike words, they do not lie—
and I was answered with circles
dead leaves uttered, falling onto a pond.

Snow was falling, sliding embarrassed
past bars where noisiness never ceases,
settling tinted on the swollen neon veins
on the city's sleepless brow,
on the incessant smile of a candidate
who was trying, not without difficulty, to get in
somewhere, I don't remember just where,
and to the snow it didn't matter where.

But in the Park it fell undisturbed:
the snowflakes descended cautiously
onto the softly sinking leaves,
soggy multicolored floats;

onto a pink and tremulous balloon
childishly fastened with chewing gum
to the trunk of an evergreen
and sleepily rubbing its cheek against the sky;
onto someone's forgotten glove,
onto the zoo, which had shown its guests out,
onto the bench with its wistful legend:
PLACE FOR LOST CHILDREN.

Dogs licked the snow in a puzzled way,
and squirrels with eyes like lost beads
flickered between cast-iron baskets,
amidst trees lost in the woods of themselves.
Great juttings of granite stood about
morosely, preserving in mineral calm
a silent question, a reproach—
lost children of former mountains.

Behind a wire fence, zebras munching hay
peered, at a loss, into striped darkness.
Seals, poking their noses from the pool,
caught snow in mid-flight on their whiskers;
they gazed around them, quizzical, confused,
forsaken children of Mother Ocean
taking pity, in their slippery style,
on people—lost children of the Earth.

I walked alone. Now and then, in the thicket,
the crimson firefly of a cigarette
floated before an unseen face—
the staring pupil of Night's wide eye.

And I felt some stranger's feeling of being lost
was searching embarrassed
for a feeling of being lost like my own,
not knowing that this was what I longed for.

At night, beneath this snowfall,
its whispered secret having made us one,
America and I sat down together
in the place for lost children.

TRANSLATED BY JOHN UPDIKE
WITH ALBERT C. TODD

MONOLOGUE OF AN AMERICAN POET

to Robert Lowell

A loved one leaves
  like air from the lungs—
vapor amid the final dry snowflakes,
the black branches clicking and sagging
  with ice.
She can't be breathed back in.
A mere gesture, I abrade my cheek
  on the rust-scaled trunk
of a drain pipe.
  To no purpose, I weep.
    She departs.
Friends depart,
  fellow sufferers,
    peers,
as from the field of the young
we are led toward separate pens
away from the once-shared milk
In vain, like an unweaned whelp,
  I whine for friends;
they don't come back.
Hopes depart—
  such darling ladies,
whom I use on such useless occasions!

Only their petticoats stay in my hands;
hopes are meant to be held for a moment.
Certitude departs.
  I remember, I swore a sacred oath
to break my stupid head against the wall
  or the wall with my stupid head.
My head is scratched, true,
  but unbroken.
And what of the wall?
  The bastard smirks;
on its blankness they are blandly changing
the posters,
  the portraits of heroes . . .
Certitude,
  where are you?
New York,
  your dark sky circles above me
    like a hawk.
America, believe me,
  I'm finished,
    I'm finished,
      finished.
I am a ship
  where all the cabins smell of doom
and rats leap in terror from the clammy deck.
Hey, seagulls—don't weep!
  Don't,
    don't pity me!
My lovely leggy guests abandon me.
They take their places, as prescribed,
  the first in the lifeboat—

Farewell, my mistresses!
My apple-cheeked cadets abandon me.
They want to live.
  Fair enough,
    they are still young.
Farewell, lads!
  Row ahead.
    You are men.
Now the inane rumble of the engine shuts down.
Only talent
  like a drunken, unshaven captain
stands somberly on the bridge.
  The captain is the captain.
But he too, tears smearing his windburned skin,
he too abandons me,
  he too . . .
    he too . . .
Hey, lifeboats—stand away!
A ship, when it sinks,
  makes a maelstrom around it.
To be totally alone
  hurts worse than a knife,
but I won't suck anyone down with me.
I forgive you all.
  Robed in death's foam,
I bequeath it you to demolish that bastardly wall.
  My trumpet juts from the marble swirls:
    comrades, battle on.

1967

TRANSLATED BY JOHN UPDIKE
WITH ALBERT C. TODD

MONOLOGUE OF A POLAR FOX ON AN ALASKAN FUR FARM

I am a blue fox on a gray farm.
Condemned to slaughter by my color
behind this gnawproof wire screen,
I find no comfort in being blue.

Lord, but I want to molt! I burn
to strip myself of myself in my frenzy;
but the luxuriant, bristling blue
seeps through the skin—scintillant traitor.

How I howl—feverishly I howl
like a furry trumpet of the last judgment,
beseeching the stars either for freedom forever,
or at least forever to be molting.

A passing visitor captured my howl
on a tape recorder. What a fool!
He didn't howl himself, but he might
begin to, if he were caught in here!

I fall to the floor, dying.
Yet somehow, I fail to die.
I stare in depression at my own Dachau
and I know: I'll never escape.

Once, after dining on a rotten fish,
I saw that the door was unhooked;
toward the starry abyss of flight I leaped
with a pup's perennial recklessness.

Lunar gems cascaded across my eyes.
The moon was a circle! I understood
that the sky is not broken into squares,
as it had been from within the cage.

Alaska's snowdrifts towered all around,
and I desperately capered, diseased,
and freedom did a Twist inside my lungs
with the stars I had swallowed.

I played pranks, I barked nonsense
at the trees. I was my own pure self.
And the iridescent snow was unafraid
that it was also very blue.

My mother and father didn't love each other,
but they mated. How I'd like
to find a girl-fox so that I could
tumble and fly with her in this sumptuous powder!

But then I'm tired. The snow is too much.
I cannot lift my sticking paws.
I have found no friend, no girl friend.
A child of captivity is too weak for freedom.

He who's conceived in a cage will weep for a cage.
Horrified, I understood how much I love
that cage, where they hide me behind a screen,
and the fur farm—my motherland.

And so I returned, frazzled and beaten.
No sooner did the cage clang shut,
than my sense of guilt became resentment
and love was alchemized again to hate.

In you, Alaska, I howled in lost despair.
In prison now, I am howling in despair.
My America, I am lost,
but who hasn't gotten lost in you?

True, there are changes on the fur farm.
They used to suffocate us in sacks.
Now they kill us in the modern mode—
electrocution. It's wonderfully tidy.

I contemplate my Eskimo-girl keeper.
Her hand rustles endearingly over me.
Her fingers scratch the back of my neck.
But a Judas sadness floods her angel eyes.

She saves me from all diseases
and won't let me die of hunger,
but I know that when the time, set firm as iron,
arrives, she will betray me, as is her duty.

Brushing a touch of moisture from her eyes,
she will ease a wire down my throat, crooning.
BE HUMANE TO THE EMPLOYEES! ON FUR FARMS
INSTITUTE THE OFFICE OF EXECUTIONER!*

I would like to be naïve, like my father,
but I was born in captivity: I am not him.
The one who feeds me will betray me.
The one who pets me will kill me.

TRANSLATED BY JOHN UPDIKE
WITH ALBERT C. TODD

* Echoing typical signs on a Soviet collective farm.

FLOWERS & BULLETS

Of course: Bullets don't like people
who love flowers.
They're jealous ladies, bullets,
short on kindness.
Allison Krause, nineteen years old,
you're dead,
for loving flowers.
When, thin and open as the pulse of conscience,
you put a flower in a rifle's mouth
and said,
"Flowers are better than bullets,"
that
was pure hope speaking.
Give no flowers to a state
that outlaws truth;
such states reciprocate
with cynical, cruel gifts,
and your gift, Allison Krause,
was the bullet
that blasted the flower.
Let every apple orchard blossom black,
black in mourning.
Ah, how the lilac smells!
You're without feeling.

Nothing. The President said it:
"You're a bum."
All the dead are bums.
It's not their crime.
You lie in the grass,
a melting candy in your mouth,
done with dressing in new clothes,
done with books.
You used to be a student.
You studied fine arts.
But other arts exist,
arts of blood and terror,
and headsmen with a genius for the axe.
Who was Hitler?
A cubist of gas chambers.
In the name of all flowers
I curse your works,
you architects of lies,
maestros of murder!
Mothers of the world whisper
"O God, God"
and seers are afraid
to look ahead.
Death dances rock-and-roll upon the bones
of Vietnam, Cambodia—
On what stage is it booked to dance tomorrow?
Rise up, Tokyo girls,
Roman boys,
take up your flowers
against the common foe.

Blow the world's dandelions
into a blizzard!
Flowers, to war!
Punish the punishers!
Tulip after tulip,
carnation after carnation,
rip out of your tidy beds in anger,
choke every lying throat
with earth and root!
Jasmine, clog
the spinning blades of mine-layers!
Nettles, boldly block the cross-hair sights,
drive your barbs into the lenses!
Of course:
Bullets are stronger than flowers.
Flowers aren't enough to overwhelm them.
Stems are too fragile,
petals are poor armor.
But if even flowers rise,
then we've had enough
of playing games with history.
Young America,
tie up the killer's hands.
Let there be an escalation of truth
to overwhelm the escalating lie
crushing people's lives!
Flowers, make war!
Defend what's beautiful!

Drown the city streets and country roads
like the flood of an army advancing
and in the ranks of people and flowers
arise, murdered Allison Krause,
the age's immortal,
Thorn-flower of protest!

1970

TRANSLATED BY LAWRENCE FERLINGHETTI
WITH ANTHONY KAHN

FREEDOM TO KILL

The Statue of Liberty's color
Grows ever more deathly pale
As, loving freedom with bullets
And taking liberty with bullets,
You shoot at yourself, America.

You can kill yourself like that!
It's dangerous to go out
Into this nightmare world,
But it's still more dangerous
To hide in the woods.

There's a smell on earth
Of a universal Dallas.
It's frightful to live
And this fright is full of shame.

Who's going to believe false fairy tales,
When behind a façade of noble ideas
The price of gun oil rises
And the price of human life falls?

Murderers attend funerals in mourning,
And become stockholders later,
And, once again,
Ears of grain filled with bullets
Wave in Texas fields.

The eyes of murderers peer out
From under hats and caps,
The steps of murderers
Are heard at every door,
And a second Kennedy falls . . .
America, save your children!
Children in other countries turn gray,
And their huts
Bombed at night
Burn in your fire
Just like your
Bill of Rights.

You promised to be
The world's conscience
But, at the brink of bottomless shame,
You're shooting not at King
But at your own conscience.
You're bombing Vietnam
And also your own honor.

When a nation's going dangerously insane
It can't be cured of its troubles
By hastily prescribed peace.

Perhaps the only way is shame.
History can't be cleaned in a laundry.
There are no such washing machines
Blood can't ever be washed away!

O where's it hiding,
The shame of the nation,
As if it were a runaway slave?
There are slaves within slaves.

There are many murderers at large.
They carry out their mob justice
And pogroms,
And Raskolnikov wanders through America,
Insane,
With a bloody axe.
O, Old Abe,
What are people doing,
Sadly understanding only one truth:
That the greatness of a tree
Can be judged only after it's cut down.

Lincoln basks in his marble chair,
Bleeding.

They're shooting at him again!
The beasts!

The stars
In your flag,
America,
Are bullet holes.

Arise from the dead,
Bullet-holed Statue of Liberty,
Murdered so often,
And speak out
Like a woman and a mother
And curse the freedom to kill.

And without wiping the blood
From your forehead,
Oh, Statue of Liberty, raise up
Your green, drowned woman's face
Against this death of freedom.

1968

TRANSLATED BY LAWRENCE FERLINGHETTI
WITH ANTHONY KAHN

SMOG

I awake in the Chelsea Hotel.
Am I dreaming?
  Is it the heat?
    I seem to see
black streams,
  cloudy black worms,
slithering into the cracks across the floor.
Galia's nightgown has become a shroud:
soot is sprinkled
  on the pale cotton
like coal on sugar.
  Cruel as a rasp,
a cough tears her chest.
  "Zhenya, I'm frightened!"
In our cell of a room,
  the odor of Dachau.
"Zhenya, sweet Zhenya,
  I'm suffocating!"
Her face becomes a martyr's,
  imitated in wax.
"Air,
  air . . ."
The window opens wide and—
  I know I'm not dreaming—

a shaggy faceless beast is in the room,
  opaque as a nimbus cloud,
    surging . . .
"Zhenya, I cannot breathe!"
Galia, my love,
  I am already half dead.
The air I gulp
  is airless.
There's no vent!
Shall we perish on one another's lips?
Give respiration each to each?
Equally we're prisoners of the smog;
it's too late.
  Both of us are poisoned,
    both of us,
and a kiss in this stench
would be mutual poisoning.
There are framed instructions
  on maples and elms:
HOW TO KISS IN GAS MASKS.
In bars, they hang the brand-new slogan:
YOU CAN BREATHE BEST
  THROUGH VODKA.
And the uptown radio
doesn't give a damn,
blaring out joyously:
"And the smog rolls on . . ."

Who comes here,
  shambling along the sidewalks

with the childlike sadness of
Marcello Mastroianni?
Miller?
  Arthur?
    Slowly he whispers to me:
"It smells of fires,
  of a witch hunt . . ."
Miller coughs,
  emaciated,
    his face a handsome hatchet.
Harshly he speaks in a spirit of prophecy:
"More inquisitions will set further fires.
Smog—
  This is the smoke of burnings to come."
Awkwardly shielding himself with his wing,
thirsting for secrets
  and weary of secrets,
gaunt as a stork
  on a house of his own books,
anxiously stands Updike with his noble beak.
"Zhenya,
  men have been cruelly duped;
the earth has been set on
the backs of nonexistent whales.
Mankind, all of it,
  is overstrained
with tension,
  like a centaur.
Biune, it neighs and brays,
chafed by its own duality.

Possibly smog
  is the furious steam
from the centaur's distended nostrils!"
Wiping the smog from his glasses,
standing amid books as if among gravestones,
Lowell spoke to me, clearing his throat,
with a lofty professorial style:
"Only ghosts and books have a sense of honor.
Of what are we ashamed?
Only of ghosts am I ashamed.
And I am a product of ghosts. I am
Alyosha Karamazov and Saint-Just together.
I believe in the vengeance of history,
in the vengeance of heaven for depravity.
Possibly smog is an ectoplasm
descended for vengeance upon the world's baseness."
Allen Ginsberg—
  cagey prophet-baboon—
thumps his hairy chest
  as a shaman thumps a tambourine:
"Darkness is coming,
  darkness!
It reeks of deepest hell.
Those who can breathe this stench
are not worth keeping alive!
When the world is a cadaver,
a cesspool of fog and chaos,
it is a sign of excellence
to sink and drown.

False ideas,
  false morality,
fuming so many years,
  have soiled
    the sky.
Brahma lets fall this slime—
you can't suck it in."
But above the smog,
above today's exhausted vapors,
Whitman's basso thunders
  like the roar of Sabaoth:
"Listen!
  It is easy to lose your breath on a precipice.
But breathe deeply,
  breathe deeply!
    Give it a try!
Inhale all together!
  You will see—
    only inhale,
and the phantom smog
  by your breathing will be swept from the sky!"
And I felt the epoch
  standing still awaiting,
like a revolution of the universe,
  our common deep breath.

TRANSLATED BY JOHN UPDIKE
WITH ALBERT C. TODD

APPENDIX

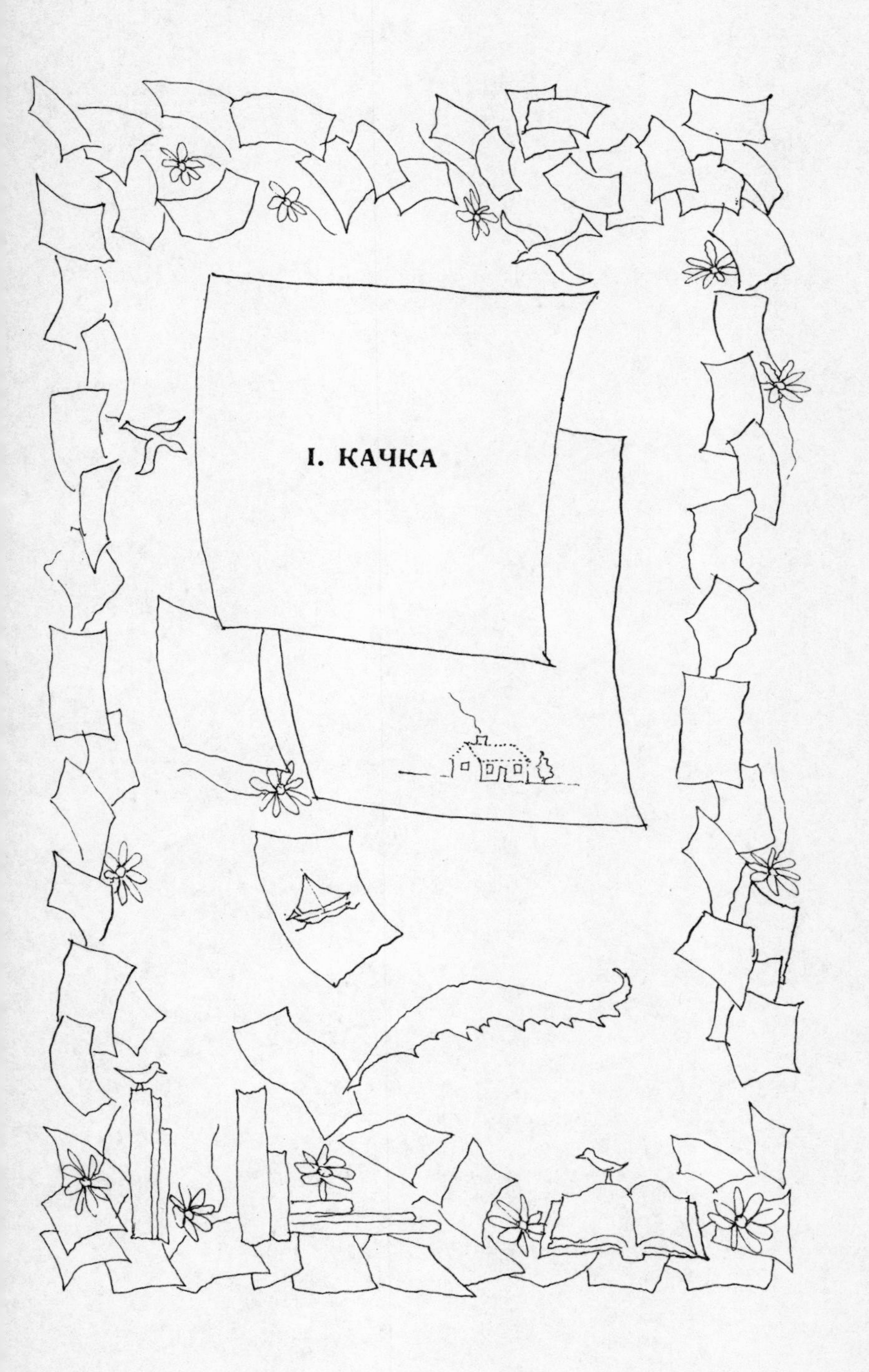

I. КАЧКА

ИЗБА

И вновь рыбацкая изба
меня впустила ночью поздней
и сразу стала так близка,
как та, где по полу я ползал.

Я потихоньку лег в углу,
как бы в моем углу извечном,
на шатком, щелистом полу,
мне до шершавинки известном.

Я здесь был свой, до боли свой,
и, возвышая, очищая,
здссь пахло рыбою, махрой,
детьми, котятами и щами.

Рыбак уже храпел вовсю.
Взобрались дети на полати,
держа в зубенках на весу
еще горячие оладьи.

И лишь хозяйка не легла.
Она то мыла, то скоблила.
Ухват, метла или игла —
в руках все время что-то было.

Печору, видно, проняло —
Печора ухала взбурленно.
«Дурит ...» — хозяйка про нее
сказала, будто про буренку.

В коптилку тусклую дохнув,
хозяйка вышла. Мгла обстала.
А за стеною — «хлюп да хлюп!» —
стирать хозяйка в кухне стала.

Кряхтели ходики в ночи —
они историю влачили.
Светились белые лучи
свеженащипанной лучины.

И, удивляясь и боясь,
из темноты неприрученно
светились восемь детских глаз
как восемь брызг твоих, Печора.

С полатей головы склоня,
из невозможно дальней дали
четыре маленьких меня
за мною, взрослым, наблюдали.

За них, молясь углами губ,
лежал я, спящим притворившись,
и вдруг затихло «хлюп да хлюп!» —
и дверь чуть-чуть приотворилась.

И ощутил я в тишине
сквозь ту притворную дремоту
сыздетства памятное мне
прикосновение чего-то.

Тулуп — а это был тулуп —
облег меня лохмато, жарко,
а в кухне снова — «хлюп да хлюп!» —
стирать хозяйка продолжала.

Сновали руки взад-вперед
в пеленках, простынях и робах
под всех страстей круговорот,
под мировых событий рокот.

И не один, должно быть, хлюст
сейчас в бессмертье лез, кривляясь,
но только это «хлюп да хлюп!»
бессмертным, в сущности, являлось.

И ощущение судьбы
в меня входило многолюдно,
как ощущение избы,
где миллионам женщин трудно,

где из неведомого дня,
им полноправно обладая,
мильоны маленьких меня
за мною, взрослым, наблюдают.

1964

ПОДРАНОК

А. Вознесенскому

Сюда, к просторам вольным, северным,
где крякал мир и нерестился,
я прилетел, подранок, селезень,
и на Печору опустился.

И я почуял всеми нервами,
как из-за леса осиянно
пахнуло льдинами и нерпами
в меня величье океана.

Я океан вдохнул и выдохнул,
как будто выдохнул печали,
и все дробинки кровью вытолкнул,
даря на память их Печоре.

Они пошли на дно холодное,
а сам я, трепетный и легкий,
поднялся вновь, крылами хлопая,
с какой-то новой силой летною.

Меня ветра чуть-чуть покачивали,
неся над мхами и кустами.
Сопя, дорогу вдаль показывали
ондатры мокрыми усами.

Через простор земель непаханых,
цветы и заячьи орешки,
меня несли на пантах бархатных
веселоглазые олешки.

Когда на кочки я присаживался, —
и тундра ягель подносила,
и клюква, за зиму прослаженная,
себя попробовать просила.

И я, затворами облязганный,
вдруг понял — я чего-то стою,
раз я такою был обласканный
твоей, Печора, добротою!

Когда-нибудь опять, над Севером,
тобой не узнанный, Печора,
я пролечу могучим селезнем,
сверкая перьями парчово.

И ты засмотришься нечаянно
на тот полет и оперенье,
забыв, что все это не чье-нибудь —
твое, Печора, одаренье.

И ты не вспомнишь, как ты прятала
меня весной, как обреченно
то оперенье кровью плакало
в твой голубой подол, Печора . . .

[*Литературная Россия*, 1963]

ТЯГА ВАЛЬДШНЕПОВ

Приготовь двустволку и взгляни:
вытянув тебе навстречу клюв,
вылетает вальдшнеп из луны,
крыльями ее перечеркнув.

Вот летит он, хоркая, хрипя ...
Но скажи, — ты знаешь, отчего
тянет его, тянет на тебя,
а твою двустволку — на него?

Он летит, и счастлив его крик.
Ты, дрожа, к двустволке приник.
Он — твой безоружный двойник.
Ты — его бескрылый двойник.

Разве ты бескрылость возместишь
выстрелом в крылатость? Дробь хлестнет,
но ведь это сам ты летишь,
это сам себя стреляешь влет ...

[*Знамя,* 1963]

НЕВЕСТА

На Печоре есть рыбак
по имени Глаша.
Говорит с парнями так:
«Глаша,
да не ваша!»
Ухажеров к ляду шлет,
сердится
серьгами.
Сарафаны себе шьет
из сиянья северного!
Не красна она, наверно,
модною прическою,
но зато в косе

не лента,
а волна печерская!
Недоступна и строга,
сети вытягает,
а глаза,
как два сига,
из-под платка сигают!
Я ходил за ней,
робея,
зачарованный,
как черемухою,
ею
зачеремленный.
Я не знал, почему
(может быть, наветно)
говорили по селу
про нее:
«Невеста».
«Чья? —
ходил я сам не свой. —
Может, выдумали?»
Рыбаки,
дымя махрой,
ничего не выдымили.
«Чья она?
Чья она?
Чья она невеста?» —
спрашивал отчаянно
у норд-веста.
Вдруг один ко мне прилип
старичок запечный,
словно тундровый гриб,
на мокре взошедший:
«Больно быстр, я погляжу.
Выставь четвертиночку —
и на блюдце положу
тайну,
как чаиночку . . .»
Пил да медлил, окаянный,
а когда все выкачал:

«Чья невеста?
                    Океана . . .
Того . . .
          Ледовитыча . . .»
Если б не был пьюха стар,
если б не был хилый,
я б манежничать не стал —
дал бы в зад бахилой!
Водят за нос меня.
Что это за шутки!
Аж гогочет гагарня,
аж хохочут щуки!

Ну, а Глаша на песке
карбас
        высмаливала,
и прорехи в паруске
на свету высматривала.
Я сказал ей:
                «Над водой
рыба вспрыгивает,
и, от криков став худой,
чернеть вскрикивает.
Хочешь — тундру подарю
лишь за взгляд за ласковый?
Горностаем подобью
ватник твой залатанный.
Пойду с неводом Печорой
в потопленные луга,
семгу выловлю,
                    в которой
не икра,
          а жемчуга.
Все сложу я,
                что захочешь,
у твоих подвернутых
у резиновых сапожек,
чешуей подернутых.
В эту чертову весну,
сам себя замучив,

я попался на блесну
зубов твоих зовучих.
Но от пьюхи-недовеска,
пьяным-пьяного,
я слыхал,
что ты невеста
океанова?!»

Отвечала Глаша:
«Да.
Я его невеста.
Видишь, как в реке вода
не находит места.
Та вода идет,
идет
к седоте глубинной,
где давно меня он ждет —
мой седой любимый.
Не подав об этом вести,
веслами посверкивая,
приплыву к нему я
вместе
с льдинками-последками.
И меня он обоймет
ночью облачною,
и в объятьях обомнет,
разом обмершую.
На груди своей держа,
все забыть поможет.
В изголовье мне
моржа
мягкого
положит.
Мне на все он даст ответ,
всплесками беседуя . . .
Что мои семнадцать лет?
С ним я,
как безлетняя.
Все семнадцать чепушинок
с меня сыплются, дрожа,
как семнадцать чешуинок

из-под вострого ножа.
Океан
то обласкает,
то грома раскатывает.
Все он гулом объясняет,
все про жизнь рассказывает.
Парень,
лучше отвяжись.
Я твоей не стану.
Что ты скажешь мне про жизнь
после океана?
Потому себя блюду,
кавалер ты липовый,
что такого не найду,
как и он,
великого . . .»
И поднялся парусок
и забился влажно,
и ушла наискосок
к океану Глаша.
Я шептал —
не помню что —
с опустелым взглядом.
Видно, слишком я не то
с океаном рядом.
И одно,
меня пронзив,
сверлит постоянно:
что же я скажу про жизнь
после океана?!

[*Юность*, 1963]

БАЛЛАДА О ЛОЖНЫХ МАЯКАХ

... и оные огни неправдивые смущают буши
рыбацкие вселением набежды обманной ...
Из старинной лоции

Нам уже наворожили столько лжи
голубые ледяные миражи.
Врали метеопророки.
Врал компас.
Бог,
неверующих нас,
видно, спас.
Сколько нищий в своей жизни медяков
столько видели мы ложных маяков!
И суденышко,
зверея от ругни,
мы вели на эти подлые огни.
Но огни от нас давали стрекача.
Киль карябался о камни, скрежеща,
и с ладоней кожу клочьями срывал
вырывающийся спятивший штурвал.
Мы затерты.
Льды суденышку-по грудь.
нам бы в бухту,
нам бы малость отдохнуть,
зацепиться ржавым якорем за дно,
подремать с водой спокойной заодно.
Но мы тычемся опять о миражи
так, что ржут соленоусые моржи.
К порошковому привыкнув молоку,
мы не верим никакому маяку.
Можно сильно в этом деле прогадать —
настоящий,
а не ложный проморгать.
Но надежней доверять не маякам —
доверять своей башке,
своим рукам.
Вот опять биноклем бодро машет кэп:
«Эй, штурвальный, вон маяк,

ты что, — ослеп?»
но штурвальный,
не впадая в его раж,
отвечает ему, хмыкнувши:
«Мираж ...»

1964 [*Юность*, 1964]

КАЧКА

Качка!
Застекленные инструкции
срываются с гвоздей.
О башку «Спидола» стукается
вместе с Дорис Дэй.
Борщ, на камбузе томящийся,
взвивается, плеща.
К потолку прилип, дымящийся,
лист лавровый из борща.
Качка!
Уцепиться бы руками
за кустарник, за траву.
Травит юнга.
Травит штурман.
Травит боцман.
Я травлю.
Волны, словно волкодавы ...
Ты такой, двадцатый век:
вправо-влево,
влево-
вправо,
вверх-вниз,
вниз-вверх.
Качка!
Все инструкции разбиты,
все портреты тоже-вдрызг.
Лица мертвенны, испиты.
под кормой-крысиный визг,

а вокруг сплошная каша,
только крики на ветру,
только качка,
качка,
качка,
только мерзостно во рту.
Качка!
Бочка прыгает но палубе,
бросаясь на людей.
Эх, ребята, и попали мы,
а все же-не робей.
Вылезайте из кают,
а не то, нам всем -каюк ...
Качка ...
А глаза у гарпунера,
чумового горлодера
напряглись,
и чуб-торчком.
Молча сделав знак матросам,
к бочке мечущейся
с тросом
подбирается бочком
и бросается, что кошка,
рассекая толчею,
ибо знает, сволочь-качка,
философию твою.
Шкурой вызубрил он, рыжий,
навсегда в башку вдолбя:
или сам на бочку прыгнешь,
или- бочка на тебя!
Качка!
А бочка смирная лежит и не блажит.
Качка!
Погода ясная от нас не убежит.
Качка!
Пусть мы закачаны, и пусть в глазах темно-
перекачаем тебя, качка,
все равн ...

[*Звезда востока*, 1966]

II. ТВИСТ НА ГВОЗДЯХ

□ □ □

Ты начисто притворства лищена,
когда молчишь со взглядом напряженным,
как лишена притворства тишина
беззвездной ночью в городе сожженном.

Он, этот город, — прошлое твое.
В нем ты почти ни разу не смеялась,
бросалась то в тряпье, то в забытье,
то бунтовала, то опять смирялась.

Ты жить старалась из последних сил,
но, отвергая все живое хмуро,
он, этот город, на тебя давил
угрюмостью своей архитектуры.

В нем изнутри был заперт каждый дом.
В нем было все недобро умудренным.
Он не скрывал свой тягостный надлом
и ненависть ко всем, кто́ не надломлен.

Тогда ты ночью подожгла его.
Испуганно от пламени метнулась,
и я был просто первым, на кого
ты, убегая, в темноте наткнулась.

Я обнял всю дрожавшую тебя,
и ты ко мне безропотно прижалась,
еще не понимая, не любя,
но, как зверек, благодаря за жалость.

И мы с тобой пошли ... Куда пошли?
Куда глаза глядят. Но то и дело
оглядывалась ты, как там, вдали,
зловеще твое прошлое горело.

Оно сгорело до конца, дотла.
Но с той поры одно меня тиранит:
туда, где неостывшая зола,
тебя как зачарованную тянет.

И вроде ты со мной, и вроде нет.
На самом деле я тобою брошен.
Неся в руке голубоватый свет,
по пепелищу прошлого ты бродишь.

Что там тебе? Там пусто и серо!
О, прошлого таинственная сила!
Ты не могла любить его само,
ну а его руины — полюбила.

Могущественны пепел и зола.
Они в себе, наверно, что-то прячут.
Над тем, что так отчаянно сожгла,
по-детски поджигательница плачет.

[*Нежность*, 1962]

□ □ □

Следов сырые отпечатки,
бульвар,
заснеженный трамвай,
прикосновение перчатки
и быстрое:
— Прощай!
Иду направленно,
мертво,
и тишина,
и снег витает.
Вот поворот,
вот вход в метро,
и яркий свет,
и шапка тает.
Стою на легком сквозняке,
смотрю в тоннель,
набитый мраком,
и трогаю рукою мрамор,
и холодно моей руке.

И шум,
            и отправлений чинность.
И понимать мне тяжело,
что ничего не получилось
и получиться не могло ...

[*Обещание*, 1956]

МАША

Вдоль моря быстро девочка проходит,
бледнея, розовея и дичась.
В ней все восходит. Что с ней происходит?
В ней возникает женщина сейчас.

Она у моря тапочки снимает,
вступает, словно в музыку, в него,
и все она на свете понимает,
хотя не понимает ничего.

Рассудок трезвый, безрассудства масса,
взгляд из-под чуткой челки через всех
и — снова вниз ... Все это вместе — Маша,
серьезный большеглазый человек.

И у меня пересыхает нёбо,
когда, забыв про чей-то взрослый суд,
мальчишеские тоненькие ноги
ее ко мне беспомощно несут.

И на сыром песке у старой лодки
целую все призывней и властней
все то, что руки Машины, — от локтя
до розоватых лепестков ногтей.

Я надеваю трубчатую маску.
Плывет и Маша где-то надо мной.

Я сквозь стекло ищу глазами Машу
среди цветов и крабов, как хмельной.

И вижу я в зеленой толще светлой
над бурою подводною грядой —
колышутся, как беленькие стебли,
мальчишеские ноги под водой.

И я плыву, плыву в подводных чащах,
плыву я, воду ластами кроя,
и я несчастлив отчего, что счастлив,
и снова счастлив, что несчастлив я.

Что мне сказать? Пусть не боится мама —
тебе не причиню я, Маша, зла.
Мне от тебя немного надо, Маша,
и очень много — чтобы ты была.

В раздумиях о вечности и смерти,
охваченный надеждой и тоской,
гляжу сквозь твое тоненькое сердце,
как сквозь прозрачный камушек морской.

Коктебель, 1958

НЕ НАДО . . .

Не надо . . .
Все призрачно —
и темных окон матовость,
и алый снег за стопсигналами машин.
Не надо . . .
Все призрачно,
как сквер туманный мартовский,
где нет ни женщин, ни мужчин —
лишь тени женщин и мужчин.

Не надо ...
Стою у дерева,
молчу и не обманываю,
гляжу,
как сдвоенные светят фонари,
и тихо трогаю рукой,
но не обламываю
сосульку тоненькую с веточкой внутри.
Не надо ...
Пусть в бултыхающемся заспанном трамваишке
с Москвой, качающейся мертвенно в окне,
ты,
подперев щеку рукою в детской варежке,
со злостью женской вспоминаешь обо мне.
Не надо ...
Ты станешь женщиной, усталой умной женщиной,
по слову доброму и ласке голодна,
и будет март,
и будет мальчик, что-то шепчущий,
и будет горестно кружиться голова.
Не надо ...
Пусть это стоит, как и мне, недешево,
с ним не броди вдвоем по мартовскому льду,
ему на плечи
свои руки ненадежные
ты не клади,
как я сегодня не кладу.
Не надо ...
Не верь, как я не верю призрачному городу,
не то, очнувшись,
ужаснешься пустырю.
Скажи: «Не надо ...», —
опустивши низко голову,
как я тебе сейчас
«не надо ...»
говорю ...

1960

□ □ □

«Нет, нет,
я не сюда попал.
Произошла нелепость.
Я ошибся.
Случаен и в руке моей бокал.
Случаен и хозяйки взгляд пушистый.
«Станцуем, а?
Ты бледен.
Плохо спал . . .»
и чувствую,
что никуда не денусь,
но говорю поспешно:
«Я оденусь.
Нет, нет, —
я не сюда попал . . .»
А вслед:
«Вот до чего вино доводит . . .
Как не сюда —
да именно сюда.
Расстроил всех собою и доволен.
С тобою просто, Женичка, беда.»

В карманы руки зябкие засовываю,
а улицы кругом снежным-снежны.
В такси ныряю.
Шеф, гони!
За Соколом
есть комнатка.
Там ждать меня должны.
Мне открывает дверь она,
но что такое с нею
и что за странный взгляд?
«Уж около пяти.
Не мог бы ты притти еще позднее?
Ну что ж, входи . . .
Куда теперь итти»

Расхохочусь,

а может быть, расплачусь?
Стишки кропал,
а вышло, что пропал.
От глаз я прячусь.
Зыбко-зыбко пячусь:
«Нет, нет —
я не сюда попал.»
И снова ночь,
и снова снег,
и чья- то песня наглая,
и чей-то чистый-чистый смех,
и закурить бы надо ...
В пурге мелькают пушкинские бесы,
и страшен их насмешливый оскал.
Страшны ларьки,
аптеки и собесы ...
Нет, нет,
я не сюда попал.
Как страшно жить,
как страшно жить, —
страшней —
уйти от жизни.
Бездомный, словно вечный жид,
эпохой я ошибся.
Нет, нет —
я не сюда попал.
Иду, сутуля плечи,
как будто что-то проиграл,
а расплатиться нечем ...

[*Знамя*, 1967]

216

□ □ □

А снег повалится, повалится,
и я прочту в его канве,
что моя молодость повадится
опять заглядывать ко мне.

И поведет куда-то за руку
на чьи-то тени и шаги,
и вовлечет в старинный заговор
огней, деревьев и пурги.

И мне покажется, покажется
по Сретенкам и Моховым,
что молод не был я пока еще,
а только буду молодым.

И ночь завертится, завертится
и, как в воронку, втянет в грех,
и моя молодость завесится
со мною снегом ото всех.

Но, сразу ставшая накрашенной
при беспристрастном свете дня,
цыганкой, мною наигравшейся,
оставит молодость меня.

Начну я жизнь переиначивать,
свою наивность застыжу
и сам себя, как пса бродячего,
на цепь угрюмо посажу.

Но снег повалится, повалится,
закружит все веретеном,
и моя молодость появится
опять цыганкой под окном.

А снег повалится, повалится,
и цепи я перегрызу,
и жизнь, как снежный ком, покатится
к сапожкам чьим-то там, внизу ...

[*Огонек*, 1966]

□ □ □

Я разлюбил тебя ... Банальная развязка,
банальная, как жизнь, банальная, как смерть.
Я оборву струну жестокого романса,
гитару пополам — к чему ломать комедь!

Лишь не понять щенку — лохматому уродцу, —
чего ты так мудришь, чего я так мудрю.
Его впущу к себе — он в дверь твою скребется,
а впустишь ты его — скребется в дверь мою.

Пожалуй, можно так с ума сойти, метаясь ...
Сентиментальный пес, ты попросту юнец,
но не позволю я себе сентиментальность.
Как пытку продолжать — затягивать конец.

Сентиментальным быть не слабость — преступленье,
когда размякнешь вновь, наобещаешь вновь
и пробуешь, кряхтя, поставить представление,
с названием тупым: «Спасенная любовь».

Спасать любовь пора уже в самом начале
от пылких «Навсегда!», от детских «Никогда!».
«Не надо обещать!» — нам поезда кричали,
«Не надо обещать!» — мычали провода.

Надломленность ветвей и неба задымленность
предупреждали нас, зазнавшихся невежд,
что полный оптимизм есть неосведомленность,
что без больших надежд — надежней для надежд.

Гуманней трезвым быть и трезво взвесить звенья
допрежь, чем их надеть, — таков закон вериг,
не обещать небес, но дать хотя бы землю,
до гроба не сулить, но дать хотя бы миг.

Гуманней не твердить «люблю», когда не любишь.
Как тяжело потом из этих самых уст
услышать звук пустой, вранье, насмешку, грубость,
и ложно полный мир предстанет ложно пуст.

Не надо обещать. Любовь — неисполнимость.
Зачем же под обман вести, как под венец!
Виденье хорошо, пока не испарилось.
Гуманней не любить, когда потом конец.

Скулит наш бедный пес до умопомраченья,
то лапой в дверь твою, то в дверь мою скребя.
За то, что разлюбил, я не прошу прощенья,
прости меня за то, что я любил тебя.

[*Огонек*, 1966]

□ □ □

В самолетах, бесстрастно новейших,
набирая, как страсть, высоту,
я летал от надежды к надежде,
убивая и эту и ту.

А надежда была посредине
вне метаний и аэровех,
словно нерпа на крошечной льдине
с грустной мордочкой, задранной вверх.

Прижимал я к губам свои губы
с горькой сладостью взлетных конфет,
но пугал, разрываясь двулюбо,
как пустой прилетевший конверт.

И звала меня бездною нежность
в шелестенье спадавших одежд,
но ввергало опять в безнадежность
прикасанье к любой из надежд.

И метался я в панике жалкой,
с перекошенной маской лица,
как собака, побитая палкой,
у которой два ложных конца.

А однажды сквозь мчание мира
я в такси увидал из окна:
у дороги стонала, как лира,
раздвоившаяся сосна.

Значит, было не так уж нелепо,
что как вечный летающий жид,
даже небо-вы слышите? — небо
я втянул в свою личную жизнь.

И прямые полетов сквозь ливни
то туда, то сюда-хоть их режь,
словно струны на стонущей лире
между двух безнадежных надежд . . .

[*Знамя,* 1967]

ТВИСТ НА ГВОЗДЯХ

Когда ты туфельки свои через плечо,
и в твист по сцене,
и пошло,
пошло,
пошло,
пусть мальчик розовый тебя и круть и верть —
так не танцует жизнь,
а так танцует смерть.
Танцуют бедра,
плечи,
груди,
локотки.
Внутри танцуют пьяно
воздуха глотки.
Танцует чье-то
на руке твоей кольцо,
и не танцует лишь одно —
твое лицо,

над жизнью тела так безжизненно летя,
как будто маска с мертвой снятая тебя.
И эта сцена —
только часть того креста,
на коем некогда
распяли Христа,
а гвозди вылезли с обратной стороны,
и танцевать на них,
торчащих,
стала ты.
И ты танцуешь на гвоздях,
на гвоздях,
на ржавых сплетнях,
на колючках-слезах,
и тем, что я тебя угрюмо полюбил,
я тоже гвозди в эту сцену
криво вбил.
Ах, сволочь-музыка,
ты все сильней, сильней?
Никто не видит —
кровь сочится из ступней.
Омыть ступни водою чистой предпочту
тебе,
Мария Магдалина, —
не Христу.
Я их отмою от сегодня и вчера
не так, как брат — сестре,
а как сестре-сестра.
Потом в руках тихонько ноги подержу
и поцелуями я их перевяжу ...

[*Знамя*, 1967]

□ □ □

Хочу того, чего сказать нельзя:
дерзя, с огнем играю без ферзя.

Мой ферзь-рассудок под ноги коню!
Какое счастье — проиграть огню!

Какой пожар в нечесаной ночи
от худенькой тебя, как от свечи!

Какого ты в понятие греха
лихого подпустила петуха!

Я корчусь, но блаженен смертный крик.
Огнем уже оправдан еретик.

В огне Гульрипш, Нью Йорк, Париж, Мадрид,
но кто-то в нем, любимый мне, горит.

А если от костра еретика
огонь скакнет на крышу бедняка, —

навеки будет проклято навзрыд
все то, за что тот еретик горит.

Ведь истина, — когда ты подожжешь
дом ближнего, — не истина, а ложь.

[*Знамя,* 1967]

222

Свет умер в зале ... Но пока играла
на сцене в главной роли темнота,
во мне была неслышимость хорала
по жилам леденяще разлита.

Я знал, что там, готовая к прологу,
и, видимая разве только богу,
как тоненький оттенок темноты,
стоишь живая, тоненькая, ты.

Мне не дал бог свой взгляд всевышний божий,
но рос хорал внутри, как божий глас,
и не глазами я смотрел, а кожей,
как тысячами слитых вместе глаз.

И в темноте, в прерывистых струеньях
дыханий чьих-то, в призрачных строеньях
теней бесплотных — чуть ли не крича,
определил я с яростным загадом
ту точку, где над раем и над адом
стояла незажженная свеча.

И ты зажглась, и свет воскрес, и хаос
чужих теней отпрянул от меня,
лишь золотая челка колыхалась,
как сбитый ветром язычок огня ...

[*Знамя,* 1967]

КРАДЕНЫЕ ЯБЛОКИ

Кренились от шторма заборы,
и крались мы в тенях озяблых,
счастливые будто бы воры
с рубахами, полными яблок.

Тяжелыми яблоки были,
и есть было страшно-престрашно,
но мы друг друга любили,
и это было прекрасно.

И нас, как сообщница пряча
от мира, где грязные волны,
шептала монахиня-дача:
«Не бойтесь любить ... Вы не воры ...»

Был дачи хозяин гуманный
футбольный на пенсии витязь,
и фото, мерцая туманно,
шептали: «Не бойтесь ... Прорвитесь ...»

И мы прорывались к воротам
в любовь, как в штрафную площадку,
и делали финт с поворотом,
и яблоками — в девятку.

И крошечны-снились нам будто —
игрушками-игрунами
качались футбольные бутсы
на ниточке тонкой над нами.

«Играйте ... — шептали, как гномы ... —
Играйте, и не понарошке ...»
и били по шару земному —
такому же, в сущности, крошке.

И мы играли и били.
Игра была, может, напрасна,
но мы друг друга любили,
и это было прекрасно.

А море, лютея от рыка,
предупреждало о чем-то,
но, как золотая рыбка,
плескалась на лбу твоем челка.

И было не боязно думать,
что в будущем, штормом закрытым,
за жадность мою и за дурость
останусь с разбитым корытом.

Пусть буду я сплетнями загнан,
я знаю — любовь не для слабых,
и запах любви — это запах
не купленных-краденых яблок.

Что крик сторожей исступленных,
когда я под брызгами моря
лежал головой на соленых
двух яблоках, краденых мною!

[*Знамя,* 1967]

□ □ □

Мне снится — я тебя уже любил.
Мне снится — я тебя уже убил.

Но ты воскресла в облике ином,
как девочка на шарике земном
в изгибисто наивной простоте
у раннего Пикассо на холсте
и попросила, ребрами моля:
«Люби меня . . .» как «Не столкни меня . . .»

Я тот усталый взрослый акробат,
от мускулов бессмысленных горбат,
который знает, что советы-ложь,
что рано или поздно упадешь.

Сказать мне страшно: «Я тебя люблю.»,
как будто выдать: «Я тебя убью.»

Ведь в глубине прозрачного лица
я вижу лица, лица без конца,
которые когда-то наповал
или не сразу — пыткой-убивал.

Ты от баланса смертного бела.
«Я знаю все — я многими была.
Я знаю — ты меня уже любил.
Я знаю — ты меня уже убил.»
Но шар земной не поверну я вспять:
люби опять, потом убей опять.»

Девчонка ты. Останови свой шар.
Я убивать устал. Я просто стар.

Но, шар земной ножонками гоня,
ты падаешь с него: «Люби меня . . .»
и лишь внутри — таких похожих! глаз
«Не убивай меня на этот раз . . .»

[*Знамя,* 1967]

Качался старый дом, в хорал слагая скрипы,
и нас, как отпевал, отскрипывал хорал.
Он чуял, дом-скрипун, что медленно и скрытно
в нем умирал ты, и я в нем умирал.

«Постойте умирать!» — звучало в ржанье с луга,
в протяжном вое псов и в сосенной волшбе,
но умирали мы навеки друг для друга,
и это все равно, что умирать вообще.

А как хотелось жить! По соснам дятел чокал,
и бешал еж ручной в усадебных грибах,

и ночь плыла, как пес, косматый, мокрый, черный,
кувшинкою речной держа звезду в зубах.

Дышала мгла в окно малиною сырою,
а за моей спиной — все видела спина! —
с платоновскою «Фро», как с найденной сестрою,
измученная мной, любимая спала.

Я думал о тупом несовершенстве браков,
О подлости всех нас — предателей, врунов.
Ведь я тебя любил, как сорок тысяч братьев,
и я тебя губил, как столько же врагов.

Какая же цена ораторскому жару,
когда, расшвырян вдрызг по сценам и клише,
хотел я счастья дать всему земному шару,
а дать его не смог одной живой душе!

Да, стала ты другой. Твой злой прищур нещаден.
Насмешки над людьми горьки и солоны.
Но кто же, как не мы, любимых превращает
в таких, каких любить уже не в силах мы!!

Да, умирали мы ... Но что-то мне мешало
уверовать в твое, в мое небытие.
Любовь еще была. Любовь еще дышала
на зеркальце в руках у слабых уст ее.

Качался старый дом, скрипел среди крапивы
и выдержку свою нам предлагал взаймы.
В нем умирали мы, но были еще живы.
Еще любили мы, но были еще живы.
Еще любили мы, и, значит, были мы.

Когда-нибудь потом — не дай мне бог, не дай мне! —
когда я разлюблю, когда и впрямь умру,
то будет плоть моя, посмеиваясь втайне:
«Ты жив!» — мне по ночам нашептывать в жару.

Но в суете страстей, печально поздний умник,
внезапно я пойму, что голос плоти лжив,
и так себе скажу: «Я разлюбил. Я умер.
Когда-то я любил. Когда-то я был жив».

[*Огонек,* 1967]

ЗАКЛИНАНИЕ

Весенней ночью думай обо мне
и летней ночью думай обо мне,
осенней ночью думай обо мне
и зимней ночью думай обо мне.
Пусть я не там с тобой, а где-то вне,
такой далекий, как в другой стране, —
на длинной и прохладной простыне
покойся, словно в море на спине,
отдавшись мягкой медленной волне,
со мной, как с морем, вся наедине.

Я не хочу, чтоб думала ты днем.
Пусть день перевернет все кверху дном,
окурит дымом и зальет вином,
заставит думать о совсем ином.
О чем захочешь, можешь думать днем,
а ночью — только обо мне одном.

Услышь сквозь паровозные свистки,
сквозь ветер, тучи рвущий на куски,
как надо мне, попавшему в тиски,
чтоб в комнате, где стены так узки,
ты жмурилась от счастья и тоски,
до боли сжав ладонями виски.

Молю тебя — в тишайшей тишине,
или под дождь, шумящий в вышине,
или под снег, мерцающий в окне,
уже во сне и все же не во сне —

весенней ночью думай обо мне
и летней ночью думай обо мне,
осенней ночью думай обо мне
и зимней ночью думай обо мне.

[*Взмах руки,* 1960]

СЕНЕГАЛЬСКАЯ БАЛЛАДА

Lannie McNulty

I

Сенегал,
я ныряю на дно кабаков
без советчиков и стукачей,
в синяках
от чумных,
начиненных нечаянностями ночей.
И плюю
на ханжей всего мира надводного —
этих и тех,
и плыву
среди стеблей подводных —
лилово мерцающих тел.
Голося,
две мулатки трясутся на сцене
и падают ниц.
Их глаза —
как актинии жадные
с щупальцами ресниц.
Но, едва
колыхаясь в чаду,
меня тянут в себя сквозь века
твои два
карих глаза,
как два необманных подводных цветка.
Мы вдвоем —
дети разных
враждующих, как у Шекспира, семей.

Белый Дом,
Серый Дом*,
мы прорвались друг к другу из ваших сетей.
Мы в ногах
у единой праматери — вечности,
гладящей головы нам.
Ланни,
лань,
ты ко мне перепрыгнула через ракеты,
эсминцы,
моря.
Где же грань,
где граница меж нами двоими? —
лишь кожа твоя и моя.
Так возьмись
перепрыгнуть и эту границу
и губы бездонные дай мне до дна.
Так вожмись
кожей в кожу,
и станут они как одна.
Ночь,
визжи!
В тебе что-то по пьянке опять,
словно атомный смерч, взорвалось,
и ножи
сумасшедшими рыбами пляшут
над водорослями волос.
Скрежеща,
стулья в воздух взлетают,
кастеты врезаются с хрустом под дых:
Страшно, а?
Режут белые — черных
и черные — белых,
а желтые — тех и других.
Рев зверья,
а над свалкой,
как будто в библейских льняных облаках,
льдом звеня,
пляшет шейкер
у бармена в цепких бесстрастных руках.

Финкой в бок
и мартелем по морде кому-то,
а бармен над хряском костей и когтей
«есть же бог!» —
наши души сбивает
в заказанный богом столетьями раньше коктейль.
Над ворьем,
над зверьем
я за руку твою осторожно берусь.
Мы вдвоем.
«Не боишься?» — глазами вопрос,
и глазами ответ: «Не боюсь».
Что мне злость
всех бандитов на свете
и что приближенье конца,
если сквозь
эту страшную драку
ко мне приближенье лица?!
Отчего
эта драка?
Какое нам дело!
А может, все эти ножи
для того,
чтобы сблизило нас
и прижало друг к другу
в крутящейся смерчем ночи.
Что любовь?
Это ты,
это я,
над кастетами,
выстрелами,
надо всем.
Что любовь?
Это вечное НАД
поножовщиной рас,
предрассудков,
сословий,
систем.
Что любовь?
Это вечное ВНЕ

всяких драк,
всяких свалок
Ромео с Джульеттой союз.
Что любовь?
«Не боишься?» — глазами вопрос,
и глазами ответ: «Не боюсь».

II

Я пришел провожать
с парой темных беспомощных рук —
не с цветами,
Мой ирландыш, прощай навсегда . . .
Ну а может . . .
А вдруг?
До свиданья!
Твое имя пребудет во мне
и в последний мой час
свято,
Ланни.
Хоть бы раз мы увиделись в жизни еще,
хоть бы раз . . .
«До свиданья!»
«Самолет на Париж,
самолет на Париж, господа!»
. . . В каравеллу
чемоданчик плывет,
как по серой реке в никуда,
по конвейеру.
Мы прижались друг к другу
затерянно, как дикари,
в тарараме
спекулянтов гашишем,
идеями,
девками,

и
даже нами.
Мы бессильны с тобой,
ну а может, мы просто малы
и безвольны?
На руках у меня,
на ногах у меня — кандалы,
лишь
без звона.
Уступаю тебя,
да и ты уступаешь меня,
как в бою
отступая ...
Кандалы на руках
и сквозь белую кожу твою
проступают.
Мы — невольники века,
невольники
наших правительств
и рас.
Всюду —
путы.
Настоящей свободы —
ее ни у нас,
ни у вас —
лишь минуты.
Отпустив на минуту,
обмякшую жертву питон
дальше
душит.
Что любовь?
Это только минута свободы.
Потом
даже
хуже.
Нету прав у людей,
кроме древнего права страдать,
но и в этом
не хотят нам свободу по выбору нашему дать
кольца века.

Век сдавил наши души и, мнимой свободой дразня,
мнет их люто.
Если вечной свободы попавшему в кольца нельзя —
пусть
        минута!
А потом —
                меня можете вешать,
                                        ножами тупыми стругать —
что угодно!
Только раньше вы дайте мне право
                                        свободно страдать,
но свободно.
Пусть нам снова страдать,
                                        если снова мы будем вдвоем —
до свиданья!
Мыслим, — значит, живем?
                                        Нет, страдаем — и, значит, живем!
До страданья!

[*Звезда востока,* 1966]

III. МУКИ СОВЕСТИ

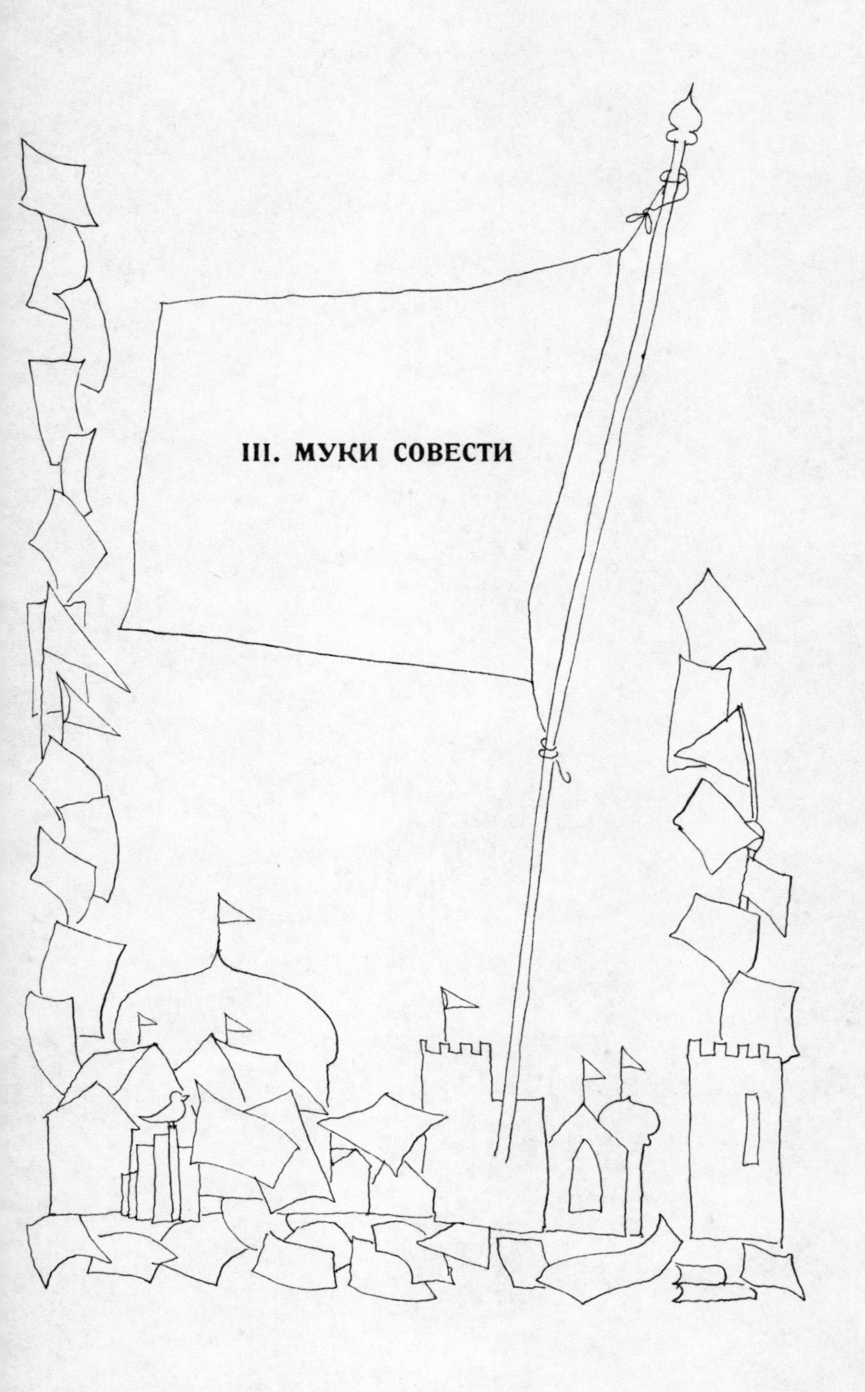

КОРОВЫ

Все в чулках речного ила
помню-тихо шли стада,
а когда все это было,
не могу сказать когда.

Масти серой, масти пегой
шли коровы под горой ...
Год был, вроде, сорок первый
или год сорок второй.

Не в хлева, не для поправки
все в репейнике, в пыли
их к вагонам для отправки
молча школьники вели.

И со всеми я, усталый,
замыкающий ряды,
шел в буденовке линялой
с темным следом от звезды.

Ах, коровы, ах, коровы,
как вносили вы в луга,
словно царские короны,
ваши белые рога.

Вы тихонечко мычали,
грустно терлись о кусты,
или попросту молчали
и роняли с губ цветы ...

А теперь — коров к вагонам
подводили, и бойцы
с видом-помню-чуть смущенным
с них снимали бубенцы.

Рядом пили, рядом пели,
но открылся свет вдали,
и вагоны заскрипели,
заскрипели и пошли.

И какой-то оробелый
с человеческим лицом
в дверь глядел теленок белый
рядом с худеньким бойцом.

Он глядел, припав к шинели,
на поля и на леса,
а глаза его синели,
как Есенина глаза ...

[*Литературная Россия,* 1961]

□ □ □

Но лишь божественный глагол ...

А. Пушкин

Поэзия чадит,
да вот не вымирает.
Поэзия чудит,
когда нас выбирает.

Вот малый не дурак,
валидой сосущий,
в портфельчике несущий
отварной бурак.
Ему сейчас бы мусса
и ромовых баб,
но Муза —
ай да Муза! —
его за шкирку
цап!

И мысли лоб сверлят,
и он забыл о ложке,
и он гигант!
Сократ!
. . . в обломовском обложке.
И вот не Аполлон —
тщедушный и невзрачный.
Весь как опенок он,
и зыбкий,
и прозрачный.
Но вдруг какой-то свист
в ушах его —
и точка!
И как боксерский свинг,
по морде века —
строчка!
А вот —
валится с ног
шалавая пичужка —
тряпичница,
пьянчужка,
салонный клоунок.
Но что-то ей велит,
и —
как зимою ветки,
бог
изнутри
звенит,
и —
мраморнеют веки.
А вот
пошляк,
шаман,
впрямь —
из шутов гороховых!
Ему —
подай шампань,
и баб —
да и не ромовых!
Но вдруг внутри приказ

прорежется сурово,
и он —
народный глас,
почти Савонарола!

Поэзия чудит,
когда нас выбирает,
а после не щадит
и души выбивает.
Но кто нам всем судья?
Да,
для мещан мы «в тлене»,
но за самих себя
мы сами —
искупленье!

ПАНОПТИКУМ В ГАМБУРГЕ

Полны величья грузного,
надменны и кургузы,
на коммуниста русского
нахмурились курфюрсты.
Все президенты,
канцлеры
в многообразной пошлости
глядят угрюмо,
кастово,
и кастовость их —
в подлости.
За то, что жизнь увечили,
корежили,
давили,
их здесь увековечили —
верней,
увосковили.
В среду заплывших,
жирных
и тощих злобных монстров

как вы попали,
Шиллер,
как вы попали,
Моцарт?
Вам бы —
в луга светающие,
вам бы —
в цветы лесные ...
Вы здесь —
мои товарищи.
Враги —
все остальные.
Враги глядят убийственно,
а для меня не гибельно,
что я не нравлюсь Бисмарку
и уж, конечно, Гитлеру.
Но вижу среди них,
как тени роковые,
врагов,
еще живых,
фигуры восковые.
Вон там —
один премьер,
вон там —
другой премьер,
и этот —
не пример,
и этот —
не пример.
Верней, примеры,
да,
но подлого,
фальшивого ...
Самих бы их сюда,
в паноптикум,
за шиворот!
Расставить по местам —
пускай их обвоскуют.
По стольким подлецам
паноптикум тоскует!

Обрыдла их игра.
Довольно врать прохвостам!
Давно пришла пора
живых,
залить их воском.
Пусть он им склеит рты,
пусть он скует им руки.
И пусть замрут,
мертвы,
как паиньки,
по струнке.
Я объявляю бунт.
Я призываю всех
их стаскивать с трибун
под общих свист и смех.
Побольше,
люди,
злости!
Пора всю сволочь смаху
из кресел,
словно гвозди,
выдергивать со смаком.
Коллекцию их рож
пора под резкий луч
выуживать из лож,
что карасей из луж.
Пора в конце концов
избавиться от хлама.
В паноптикум
лжецов —
жрецов из храма срама!
Подайте,
люди,
глас —
не будьте же безгласны!
В паноптикум —
всех глав,
которые безглавы!
И если кто-то врет —

пусть даже и по-новому,
вы —
восском ему в рот:
в паноптикум!
в паноптикум!
Еще полно дерьма,
лжецов на свете —
войско ...
Эй, пчелы,
за дела!
Нам столько надо воска!

ГЛУБИНА

Будил захвоенные дали
рев парохода поутру,
а мы на палубе стояли
и наблюдали Ангару.
Она летела озаренно,
и дно просвечивало в ней
сквозь толщу волн светло-зеленых
цветными пятнами камней.
Порою, если верить глазу,
могло казаться на пути,
что дна легко коснешься сразу,
лишь в воду руку опусти.
Пусть было здесь немало метров,
но так вода была ясна,
что оставалась неприметной
ее большая глубина.
Я знаю: есть порой опасность
в незамутненности волны —
ведь ручейков журчащих ясность
отнюдь не признак глубины.
Но и другое мне знакомо,
и я не ставлю ни во грош
бессмысленно глубокий омут,

где ни черта не разберешь.
И я хотел бы стать волною
реки, зарей пробитой вкось,
с неизмеримой глубиною
и с каждым
камешком
насквозь!

[*Третий, снег* 1952]

МУКИ СОВЕСТИ

Д. Шостаковичу

Мы живем, умереть не готовясь,
забываем поэтому стыд,
но мадонной невидимой совесть
на любых перекрестках стоит.

И бредут ее дети и внуки
при бродяжьей клюке и суме —
муки совести — странные муки
на бессовестной к стольким земле.

От калитки опять до калитки,
от порога опять на порог
они странствуют, словно калики,
у которых за пазухой — бог.

Не они ли с укором бессмертным
тусклым ногтем стучали тайком
в слюдяные окошечки смердов,
а в хоромы царей — кулаком?

Не они ли на загнанной тройке
мчали Пушкина в темень пурги,
Достоевского гнали в остроги
и Толстому шептали: «Беги!»

Палачи понимали прекрасно:
«Тот, кто мучится, — тот баламут.
Муки совести — это опасно.
Выбьем совесть, чтоб не было мук».

Но как будто набатные звуки,
сотрясая их кров по ночам,
муки совести — грозные муки —
проникали к самим палачам.

Ведь у тех, кто у кривды на страже,
кто давно потерял свою честь,
если нету и совести даже —
муки совести вроде бы есть.

И покуда на свете на белом,
где никто не безгрешен, никто,
в ком-то слышится: «Что я наделал?»,
можно сделать с землей кое-что.

Я не верю в пророков наитья,
во второй или в тысячный Рим,
верю в тихое «Что вы творите?»,
верю в горькое «Что мы творим?».

И целую вам темные руки
у безверья на скользком краю,
муки совести, светлые муки
за последнюю веру мою.

1966

[*Огонек*, 1967]

ПАМЯТИ АХМАТОВОЙ

I

Ахматова двувременной была.
О ней и плакать как-то не пристало.
Не верилось, когда она жила,
не верилось, когда ее не стало.

Она ушла, как будто бы напев
уходит в глубь темнеющего сада.
Она ушла, как будто бы навек
вернулась в Петербург из Ленинграда.

Она связала эти времена
в туманно-теневое средоточье,
и если Пушкин — солнце, то она
в поэзии пребудет белой ночью.

Над смертью и бессмертьем, вне всего,
она лежала, как бы между прочим,
не в настоящем, а поверх него,
лежала между будущим и прошлым.

И прошлое у гроба тихо шло
не вереницей дам богоугодных.
Седые челки гордо и светло
мерцали из-под шляпок старомодных.

Да, изменило время их черты,
красавиц той, когдатошней России,
но их глаза — лампады доброты —
ни круговерть, ни мгла не загасили.

Шло будущее, слабое в плечах.
Шли мальчики. Они себя сжигали
пожаром гимназическим в очах
и в кулаках тетрадочки сжимали.

И девочки в портфельчиках своих
несли, наверно, дневники и списки.

Все те же — из блаженных и святых —
наивные российские курсистки.

И ты, распад всемирный, не убий
ту связь времен, — она еще поможет:
Ведь просто быть не может двух Россий,
как быть и двух Ахматовых не может.

II

Ну, а в другом гробу, невдалеке,
как будто рядом с библией частушка,
лежала в белом простеньком платке
ахматовского возраста старушка.

Лежала, как готовилась к венцу,
устав стирать, мести, скрести и штопать,
крестьянка по рукам и по лицу,
а в общем, домработница, должно быть.

Быть мертвой — это райское житье.
За ней так добро люди приглядели
и словно перед праздником дите
и вымыли и чисто приодели.

Цветами ее, правда, не почли,
но был зато по мерке гроб подогнан,
и дали туфли новые почти,
с квиточками ремонта на подошвах.

Была она прощающе ясна
и на груди благоговейно сжала
сухие руки, будто бы она
невидимую свечку в них держала.

Они умели в жизни все уметь
писали, правда, только закорюки,
тяжелые и темные, как медь,
ни разу не целованные руки.

И думал я: а может быть, а вдруг,
но все же существуют две России:
Россия духа и Россия рук —
две разные страны, совсем чужие?!

Никто о той старушке не скорбел.
Никто ее в бессмертные не прочил.
И был над нею отстраненно бел
Ахматовой патрицианский профиль.

Ахматова превыше всех осанн
покоилась презрительно и сухо,
осознавая свой духовный сан
над самозванством и плебейством духа.

Аристократка! Вся оттуда, где
под рысаками билась мостовая!
Но руки на цветах, как на воде,
покачивались, что-то выдавая.

Они творили, как могли, добро,
но силы временами было мало,
и, легкое для Пушкина, перо
с усмешкой пальцы женские ломало.

Забыли пальцы холодок Аи,
и поцелуи в Ницце, Петербурге,
и, на груди сведенные, они
крестьянскою усталостью набухли.

Царица без короны и жезла,
среди даров почтительности тусклых,
была она прощающе ясна,
как та старушка в тех дареных туфлях.

Ну, а старушка в том, другом гробу
лежала, не увидевшая Ниццы,
с ахматовским величием на лбу,
и между ними не было границы.

[*Юность*, 1966]

ШУТЛИВОЕ

Меняю славу на бесславье,
ну, а в президиуме стул
на место теплое в канаве,
где хорошенько бы заснул.
Уж я бы выложил всю душу,
всю мою смертную тоску
вам, лопухи, в седые уши,
пока бы ерзал на боку.
И я проснулся бы, небритый,
средь вас, букашки-мураши,
ах, до чего ж незнаменитый —
ну хоть «Цыганочку» пляши.
Вдали бы кто-то рвался к власти,
держался кто-нибудь за власть,
а мне-то что до той напасти, —
мне из канавы не упасть.
И там в обнимку с псом лишайным
в такой приятельской пыли
я все лежал бы и лежал бы
на высшем уровне — земли.
И рядом плыли бы негрешно
босые девичьи ступни,
возы роняли бы небрежно
травинки бледные свои.
... Швырнет курильщик со скамейки
в канаву смятый коробок,
и мне углами губ с наклейки
печально улыбнется Блок.

[*Огонек*, 1966]

ЭСТРАДА

Проклятие мое,
души моей растрата —
эстрада ...

Я молод был.
Хотел на пьедестал,
хотел аплодисментов и букетов,
когда я вышел
и неловко стал
на тальке, что остался от балеток.
Мне было еще нечего сказать,
а были только звон внутри
и горло,
но что-то сквозь меня такое перло,
что невозможно сценою сковать.
И голосом ломавшимся моим
ломавшееся время закричало,
и время было мной,
и я был им,
и что за важность,
кто был кем сначала.
И на эстрадной огненной черте
вошла в меня невысказанность залов,
как будто бы невысказанность зарев,
которые таились в темноте.
Эстрадный жанр перерастал в призыв,
и оказалась чем-то третьим слава.
Как в библии,
вначале было слово,
ну, а потом —
сокрытый в слове взрыв.
Какой я Северянин,
дураки!
Слабы, конечно, были мои кости,
но на лице моем
сквозь желваки
прорезывался грозно Маяковский.
И, золотая вся от удальства,

дыша пшеничной ширью полевою,
Есенина шальная голова
всходила над моею головою.
Учителя,
я вас не посрамил,
и вам я тайно все букеты отдал.
Нам
вместе
аплодировал весь мир:
Париж, и Гамбург,
и Мельбурн,
и Лондон.
Но что со мной ты сделала —
ты рада,
эстрада?!
Мой стих не распустился,
не размяк,
но стал грубей и темой
и отделкой.
Эстрада,
ты давала мне размах,
но отбирала таинство оттенков.
Я слишком от натуги багровел.
В плакаты влез
при хитрой отговорке,
что из большого зала акварель
не разглядишь,
особенно с галерки.
Я верить стал не в тишину —
в раскат,
но так собою можно пробросаться.
Я научился вмазывать,
врезать,
но разучился тихо прикасаться.

И было кое-что еще страшней:
когда в пальтишки публика влезала,
разбросанный по тысячам людей,
сам от себя

я уходил из зала.
А мой двойник,
от пота весь рябой,
сидел в гримерной,
конченный волщебник,
тысячелик
от лиц, в него вошедших,
и переставший быть самим собой . . .
За что такая страшная награда —
эстрада?
«Прощай, эстрада . . .» —
тихо прошепчу,
хотя забыл я, что такое шепот.
Уйду от шума в шелесты и шорох,
прижмусь березке к слабому плечу,
но, помощи потребовав моей,
как требует предгрозье взрыва,
взлома,
невысказанность далей и полей
подкатит к горлу,
сплавливаясь в слово.

Униженность и мертвых и живых
на свете,
что еще далек до рая,
потребует,
из связок горловых
мой воспаленный голос выдирая.
Я вас к другим поэтам не ревную.
Не надо ничего — я все отдам,
и глотку
да и голову шальную,
лишь только б лучше в жизни было вам!
Конечно, будет ясно для потомков,
что я —
увы! —
совсем не идеал,
а все-таки,
пусть грубо или тонко,
но чувства добрые я лирой пробуждал.

И прохриплю,
когда иссякших сил,
пожалуй, и для шепота не будет:
«Эстрада,
я уж был какой я был,
а так ли жил —
пусть бог меня рассудит».
И я сойду во мглу с тебя без страха,
эстрада ...

[*Огонек,* 1966]

ИДОЛ

Среди сосновых игол
в завьюженном логу
стоит эвенский идол,
уставившись в тайгу.

Надменно щуря веки,
смотрел он до поры,
как робкие эвенки
несли ему дары.

Несли унты и малицы,
несли и мед и мех,
считая, что он молится
и думает за всех.

В уверенности темной,
что он их всех поймет,
оленьей кровью теплой
намазывали рот.

А что он мог, обманный
божишка небольшой,
с жестокой, деревянной,
источенной душой?

Глядит сейчас сквозь ветви,
покинуто, мертво.
Ему никто не верит,
не молится никто.

Но чудится мне? ночью
в своем логу глухом
он зажигает очи,
обсаженные мхом.

И, вслушиваясь в гулы,
пургою заметен,
облизывает губы
и крови хочет он . . .

[*Нежность*, 1955]

СТАРЫЙ БУХГАЛТЕР

Никакой не ведаю я муки,
ни о чем ненужном не сужу.
Подложив подушечку под брюки,
в черных нарукавниках сижу.

Вижу те же подписи, печати . . .
На столе бумаги шелестят,
шелестят устало и печально,
шелестят, что скоро шестьдесят.

Ах, начальник — молод он и крепок!
Как всегда, взыскательно побрит,
он, играя четками из скрепок,
про футбол со мною говорит.

Ах, начальник! — вроде бы он ччстый,
вроде не похож на подлеца,
но я вижу все, что скрыть он тщится
под сияньем гладкого дица.

Ах, начальник! — как себя он холит!
Даже перстни носит на руках!
Только он не очень твердо ходит
в замшевых красивых башмаках!

Выйду я из маленькой конторы,
улыбнусь растерянно весне
и поеду в поезде, который
до Мытищ и далее везде.

Там живут четыре, тоже старых
женщины печальных у реки.
У одной из них, таких усталых,
попрошу когда-нибудь руки.

А когда вернусь в свою каморку,
в пахнущую «Примой» тишину,
из большого ветхого комода
выну фотографию одну.

Там, неловко очень подбоченясь,
у эпохи грозной на виду,
я стою, неюный ополченец
в сорок первом искреннем году.

Я услышу самолетов гулы,
выстрелы и песни на ветру,
и прошепчут что-то мои губы,
ну а что — и сам не разберу.

1958

[*Нежность*, 1958]

ТАЙНЫ

Тают отроческие тайны,
как туманы на берегах . . .
Были тайнами — Тони, Тани,
даже с цыпками на ногах.

Были тайнами звезды, звери,
под осинами стайки опят,
и скрипели таинственно двери —
только в детстве так двери скрипят.

Возникали загадки мира,
словно шарики изо рта
обольстительного факира,
обольщающего неспроста.

Оволшебленные снещинки
опускались в полях и лесах.
Оволшебленные смешинки
у девчонок плясали в глазах.

Мы таинственно что-то шептали
на таинственном льду катка,
и пугливо, как тайна к тайне,
прикасалась к руке рука . . .

Но пришла неожиданно взрослость.
Износивший свой фрак до дыр,
в чье-то детство, как в дальнюю область,
гастролировать убыл факир.

Мы, как взрослые, им забыты.
Эх, факир, ты плохой человек.
Нетаинственно до обиды
нам на плечи падает снег.

Где вы, шарики колдовские?
Нетаинственно мы грустим.
Нетаинственны нам другие,
да и мы нетаинственны им.

Ну, а если рука случайно
прикасается, гладя слегка,
это только рука, а не тайна,
понимаете — только рука!

Дайте тайну простую-простую,
тайну — робость и тишину,
тайну худенькую, босую ...
Дайте тайну — хотя бы одну!

1960

Играла девка на гармошке.
Она была пьяна слегка,
корка черная горбушки
иоснилась вся от чеснока.

И безо всяческой героики,
в избе устроив пир горой,
мои товарищи-геологи,
обнявшись, пели под гармонь.

У ног студентки-практикантки
сидел я около скамьи.
Сквозь ее пальцы протекали
с шуршаньем волосы мои.

Я вроде пил, и вроде не пил,
и вроде думал про свое,
и для нее любимым не был,
и был любимым для нее.

Играла девка на гармошке,
о жизни пела кочевой,
и шлепали ее галошки,
прихваченные бечевой.

Была в гармошке одинокость,
тоской обугленные дни
и беспредельная далекость,
плетни, деревья и огни.

Играла девка, пела девка,
и потихоньку до утра
по-бабьи плакала студентка —
ее ученая сестра ...

1955

[*Новый мир*, 1955]

КАИНОВА ПЕЧАТЬ

Памяти Р. Кеннеди

Брели паломники сирые
в Мекку
 по серой Сирии.
Скрюченно и поломанно
передвигались паломники.
От наваждений
 и хаоса —
 каяться,
 каяться,
 каяться.
А я стоял на вершине
грешником
 нераскаянным,
где некогда —
 не ворошите! —

Авель убит был Каином.
И — самое чрезвычайное
из всех сообщений кровавых,
слышалось изначальное:
«Каин,
где брат твой, Авель?»
Но вдруг —
голоса фарисейские,
фашистские,
сладко-злодейские:
«Что вам виденья отжитого?
Да, перегнули с Авелем.
Конечно, была ошибочка,
но, в общем-то, путь был правилен . . .»
И мне представился каменный
угрюмый детдом,
где отравленно
кормят детеныши каиновы
с ложечки ложью —
авелевых.
И проступает,
алая,
когда привыкают молчать,
на лицах детей Авеля
каинова печать.

Так я стоял на вершине
меж праотцев и потомков
над миром,
где люди вершили
растленье себе подобных.
Безмолнийно было,
безгромно,
но камни взывали ребристо:
«Растление душ бескровно,
но это —
братоубийство».

А я на вершине липкой

стоял,
ничей не убийца,
но совесть библейской уликой
взывала:
«Тебе не укрыться!
Твой дух растлеваешь ты ложью,
и дух крошится,
дробится.
Себя убивать —
это тоже
братоубийство.
А скольких женщин
ты сослепу
в пути растоптал,
как распятья.
Ведь женщины —
твои сестры,
а это больше, чем братья.
И чьи-то серые,
карие
глядят на тебя
без пощады,
и вечной печатью каиновой
ко лбу прирастают взгляды . . .
Что стоят гусарские тосты
за женщин?
Бравада, отписка . . .
Любовь убивать —
это тоже
братоубийство . . .»
Я вздрогнул:
«Совесть, потише . . .
Ведь это же несравнимо,
как сравнивать цирк для детишек
с кровавыми цирками Рима . . .»

Но тень изможденного Каина
возникла у скал угловато,
и с рук нескончаемо капала
кровь убиенного брата.

«Взгляни —
мои руки кровавы.
А начал я с детской забавы.
Крылья бабочек бархатных
ломал я из любопытства.
Все начинается с бабочек.
После —
братоубийство ...»

И снова сказала,
провидица,
с пророчески-горькой печалью
совесть моя —
хранительница
каиновой печати:
«Что вечности звездной, безбрежной
ты скажешь,
на суд ее явленный?
«Конечно же, я не безгрешный,
но, в общем-то, путь мой правилен»?
Ведь это возводят до истин
все те, кто тебе ненавистен,
и человечиной жженой
«винстоны» пахнут
и «кенты»,
и пуля,
пройдя сквозь Джона,
сражает Роберта Кеннеди.
И бомбы землю бодают,
сжигая деревни пламенем.
Конечно, в детей попадают,
но, в общем-то, путь их правилен ...
Каин во всех таится
и может вырасти тайно.
Единственное убийство
священно —
убить в себе Каина!»

И я на вершине липкой
у вечности перед ликом
разверз мою грудь неприкаянно,
душа
        в зародыше
                                Каина.
Душил я все подлое,
                                злобное,
все то, что может быть подло,
но крылья бабочек сломанные
соединить было поздно.
А ветер хлестал наотмашь,
невидимой кровью намокший,
как будто страницы Библии
меня
        по лицу
                били . . .

[*Огонек,* 1968]

БАЛЛАДА О СМЕРТНИКЕ

И я вздрогну,
                        и я опомнюсь —
в стол зеленый локтями врыт,
бывший летчик-смертник —
                                        японец
о Раскольникове говорит.
На симпозиуме о романе
он,
    в свои сорок пять,
                                старик.
Он,
    как вежливое рыданье.
Он,
    как сдавленный галстуком крик.
И сквозь нас и куда-то мимо,
сквозь шимозы и тень Лазо

желтым отблеском Хиросимы,
проплывает,
кренясь,
лицо.
Ну а в горле его
то ли комья слез,
то ли комья кашля ...
Император хотел, чтобы с детства он рос
смирным смертником —
комикадзе.
Хорошо по рукам и букетам плыть,
поздравляемым быть перед строем ...
Да,
красиво народным героем быть,
но во имя чего —
героем?
И бежал из героев он с горсткой друзей,
предпочтя свою славу покинуть
и остаться в живых ...
Это было смелей
чем во имя неправды погибнуть!
Ну а я —
я слыву, что я смелый ...
Но о жизни и смерти моей
что я думаю,
грешный и смертный,
среди грешных и смертных людей?
Все мы смертники.
Все камикадзе.
Ветер смерти свистит в ушах.
Каждый шаг по планете комкастой
это к смерти невидимой шаг.
Пусть я буду разбитым и смятым —
не за то, что хотел бы тиран,
рычаги
вырывая
с мясом,
я пойду
на последний таран.
Но тогда я хотел бы, потомки,

чтоб сквозь тело истлевшее,
сквозь
моего самолета обломки
что-то доброе к вам прорвалось.
Но как страшно
себе же казаться
погибающим в небе не зря,
а, погибнув уже,
оказаться
обманувшимся смертником зла ...

[*Звезда востока*]

ПОПЫТКА БОГОХУЛЬСТВА

Обращаясъ к вечному магниту
в час, когда в душе моей ни зги,
я всегда шепчу одну молитву:
«Господи, прости и помоги ...»

И господь прощает, помогает,
разводя руками оттого,
как людское племя помыкает
милостями столькими его.

Видно, бог на нас глядит со страхом.
Как бы его кто ни называл, —
Иеговой, Буддой и Аллахом —
он один, и богом быть устал.

Будь он даже некая бестелость
или портативный идолок,
как от поцелуев бы хотелось
спрятаться в укромный уголок!

Только ему прятаться негоже,
и, согбенный, будто в рабстве негр,
хочет бог поверить в бога тоже,
но для бога в мире бога нет.

И когда с просьбишками мы липнем,
забывая отдавать долги,
некому шептать ему молитву:
«Господи, прости и помоги . . .»

[*Знамя*, 1967]

У ВОЕНКОМАТА

Под колыбельный рокот рельсов
усталой смазчицей экспрессов
дремала станция Зима.
Дремал и шпиль на райсовете,
дремал и пьяница в кювете
и сторож у «Заготзерна».

Совсем зиминский, не московский
я шел и шел, дымя махоркой,
сквозь шелест листьев, чьи-то сны.
Дождь барабанил чуть по жести . . .
И вдруг я вздох услышал женский:
«Ах, только б не было войны! . . .»

Луна скользнула по ометам,
крылечкам, ставням и заплотам,
и, замеревши на ходу,
я, что-то вещее почуя,
как тень печальную ночную,
увидел женщину одну.

Она во всем, что задремало,
чему-то тайному внимала.
Ей было лет уже немало —
не меньше чем за пятьдесят.
Она особенно, по-вдовьи
перила трогала ладонью
под блеклой вывеской на доме:
«Зиминский райвоенкомат».

Должно быть, шла она с работы,
и вдруг ее толкнуло что-то
неодолимо, как волна,
к перилам этим ... В ней воскресла
война без помпы и оркестра,
кормильца, взявшая война.
Вот здесь, опершись о перила,
об эти самые перила,
молитву мужу вслед творила,
а после шла, дитем тяжка,
рукою правою без силы
опять касаясь вас, перила,
а в левой мертвенно, остыло
бумажку страшную держа.
Ах, только б не было войны!
(была в руках его гармошка ...)
Ах, только б не было войны ...
(... была за голенищем ложка ...)
Ах, только б не было войны!
(... и на губах махорки крошка ...)
Ах, только б не было войны!
(... Шумел, подвыпивший немножко:
«Ничо, не пропадет твой Лешка!»
Ну, а в глазах его сторожко
глядела боль из глубины ...)
Ах, только б не было войны!

□ □ □

Проклятье века — это спешка,
и человек, стирая пот,
по жизни мечется, как пешка,
попав затравленно в цейтнот.

Поспешно пьют, поспешно любят,
и опускается душа.
Поспешно бьют, поспешно губят,
а после каются, спеша.

Но ты хотя б однажды в мире,
когда он спит или кипит,
остановись, как лошадь в мыле,
почуяв пропасть у копыт.

Остановись на полдороге,
доверься небу, как судье,
подумай — если не о боге —
хотя бы просто о себе.

Под шелест листьев обветшалых,
под паровозный хриплый крик
пойми: забегавшийся — жалок,
остановившийся — велик.

Пыль суеты сует сметая,
ты вспомни вечность наконец,
и нерешительность святая
вольется в ноги, как свинец.

Есть в нерешительности сила,
когда по ложному пути
вперед на ложные светила
ты не решаешься идти.

Топча, как листья, чьи-то лица,
остановись! Ты слеп, как Вий.
И самый шанс остановиться
безумством спешки не убий.

Когда шагаешь к цели бойко,
как по ступеням, по телам,
остановись, забывший бога, —
ты по себе шагаешь сам!

Когда тебя толкает злоба
к забвенью собственной души,
к бесчестью выстрела и слова, —
не поспеши, не соверши!

268

Остановись, идя вслепую,
о население Земли!
Замри, летя из кольта, пуля,
и, бомба, в воздухе замри!

О человек, чье имя свято,
подняв глаза с молитвой ввысь,
среди распада и разврата
остановись, остановись!

1968

[*Огонек*, 1968]

IV. ПРОЦЕССИЯ С МАДОННОЙ

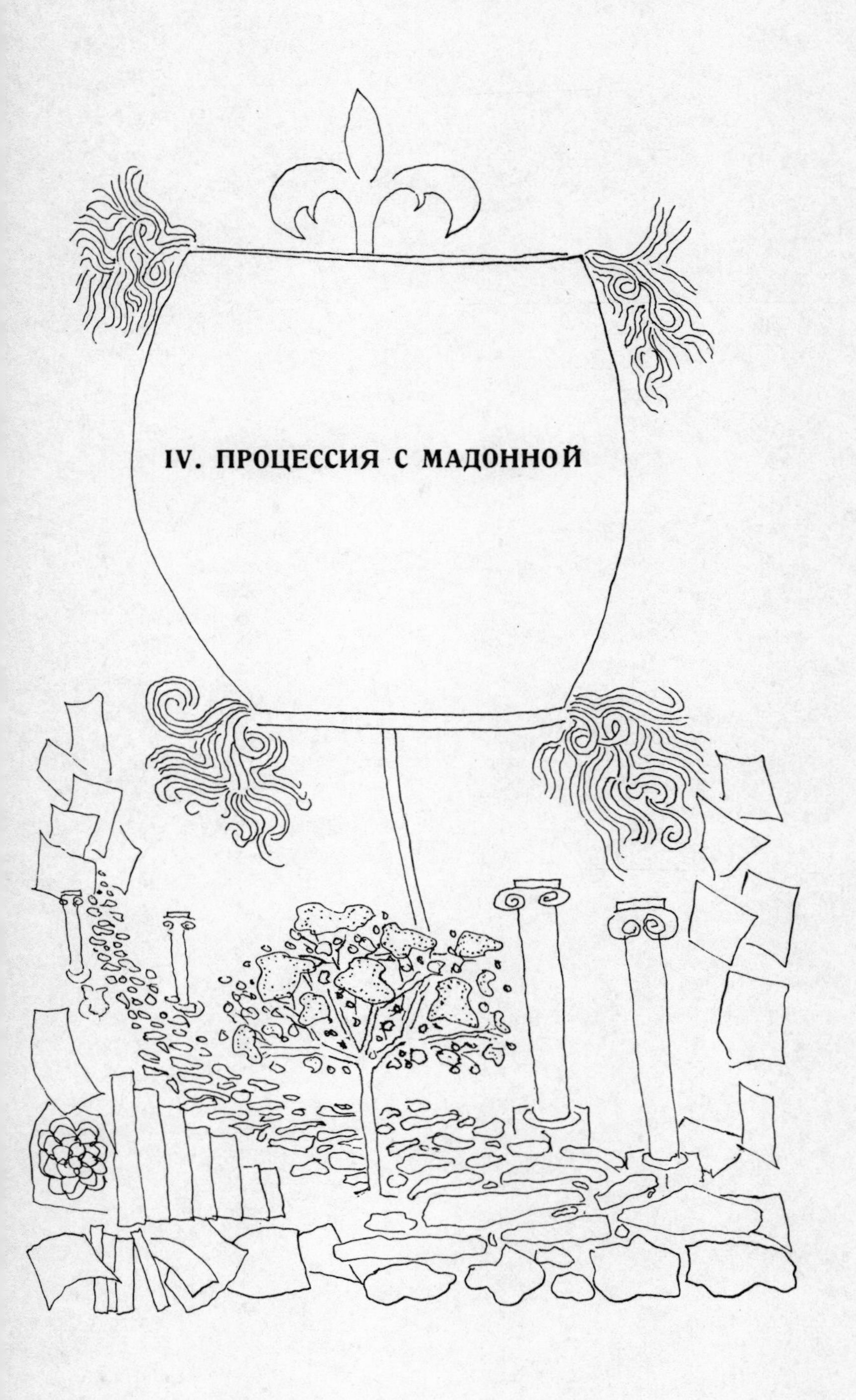

ИСПОВЕДАЛЬНЯ

Окошечко исповедальни ...
Туда, во благостную тьму
потертый лик испитой дамы
с надеждой тянется к нему.

Дитя неапольских окраин
в сторонке очереди ждет,
раскрытой библией скрывая
свой недвусмысленный живот.

Без карабина и фуражки
карабинер пришел на суд,
и по спине его мурашки
под формой грозною ползут.

Несут хозяйки от лоханей,
от ипподромов игроки
и то, что кажется грехами
и настоящие грехи.

А где моя исповедальня?
Куда приду, смиряя страх,
с греховной пылью, с пылью дальней
на заблудившихся стопах?

Я позабуду праздность, леность.
Скажите адрес — я найду.
Но исповедоваться лезут
уже ко мне, как на беду.

Чему научит исповедник
заблудших, совестью больных,
когда и сам он из последних
пропащих грешников земных?

Мы ближним головы морочим,
когда с грехами к нам бегут.
Но говорят, что люди, впрочем
вовсю на исповедях лгут.

И проповедник, это зная,
и сам спасительно им лжет,
и ложь уютная, двойная
уютно нежит, а не жжет.

Но верить вере я не вправе,
хоть лоб о плиты разможжи,
когда почти как правда правде,
ложь исповедуется лжи.

Неаполь-Москва

[*Юность*, 1965]

ЖАРА В РИМЕ

Монахи,
к черту все сутаны,
ныряйте в римские фонтаны!
А ну,
синьор премьер-министр,
скорее к По
и прямо — вниз!
И как ослы
и как ослихи,
к воде — послы,
к воде — послихи.
Миллионер,
кричи в смятеньи:
«Подайте на кусочек тени!»
Объедини хоть раз господ
с простым народом
общий пот!
Все пропотело —
даже чувства.
Газеты — липкое белье.
Мадонна плачет ...
Чудо!
Чудо!

Не верьте —
катит пот с нее.
За сорок ...
Градусники лопаются.
Танцует пьяно ртуть в пыли,
как будто крошечные глобусы,
с которых страны оползли.
Все расползается на части,
размякло все —
и даже власти.
Отщипывайте
мрамор храма
и жуйте
вместо чуингама.

А бронзовые властелины,
герои,
боги —
жалкий люд,
как будто бы из пластилина:
ткнешь пальцем —
сразу упадут.
На Пьяцца ди Индепеденца
тону беспомощней младенца.
Асфальт расплавленный —
по грудь.
«Эй, кто-нибудь!
Эй, кто-нибудь!»
Но нет —
никто не отвечает.
Жить независимо —
включает
и независимо тонуть.
А надо всем
поэт-нудист
стихи пророчески нудит:
«Коровы на лугах протухли,
на небе Млечный Путь прокис.
Воняют люди и продукты.
Спасенье —

массовый стриптиз!
Не превращайтесь, люди,
в трупы,
не бойтесь девственной красы.
Одежду носят только трусы.
Снимайте радостно трусы!»

Дамы стонут:
«Озона . . .
Озона!»
Объявили,
портных окрыля,
наимодным платьем сезона
платье голого короля.

«Ха-ха-ха! . . . —
из веков раздается ответ. —
Оно самое модное —
тысячи лет . . .»

«О депутат наш дорогой,
вы в села —
даже ни ногой,
а села обнищали . . .
Где все, что обещали?» —
«Я обещал?
Ах, да,
ах, да! . . .
Забыл —
простите, духота . . .» —
«Что ты слаб, мой миленький?
Подкрепить вином?
Ляжем в холодильнике,
может, выйдет в нем . . .»
Депутаты перед избирателями,
импотенты перед супружницами,
убийцы перед прокурорами,
адвокаты перед убийцами
все оправдываются добродушно:
«Душно . . .»

Душно,
душно ото лжи . . .
Россия,
снега одолжи!
Но ходят слухи — ну и бред! —
что и в России снега нет.
И слухи новые
Рим облетели,
что и на полюсе нету льдин,
что тлеют книги
в библиотеках,
в музеях
краски
текут
с картин
И не спит изнывающий город ночей.
Надо что-то немедля решать,
если даже и те,
кто дышал ничем,
заявляют:
«Нечем дышать!»
Из кожи мира —
грязный жир.
Провентилировать бы мир!
Все самолеты,
ракеты,
эсминцы,
все автоматы,
винтовки,
а с ними
лживый металл в голосах у ораторов,
медные лбы проигравшихся глав
на вентиляторы, —
на вентиляторы,
на вентиляторы —
в переплав!
Быть может,
поможет . . .

[*Юность*, 1966]

РИТМЫ РИМА

Вставайте,
гигантским будильником Рим тарахтит у виска.
Взбивайте
шипящую пену пушистым хвостом помазка.
И — к Риму!
Отдайтесь рассветному стуку его башмаков,
молотков
и крику
молочниц, газетчиков, пекарей, зеленщиков.
Монашки,
хрустя белокрыльем крахмальным, гуськом семенят.
Медяшки
в их глиняных кружках, взывая к прохожим,
звенят.
Путаны
идут с профилактики прямо — молиться в собор.
Пузаны
в кафе обсуждают, как вылечить лучше запор.
Монисты
бренчат на цыганках у выставки «Супер-поп-арт».
Министры
летят в «мерседесах». Ладони — в мозолях от карт.
Ладони
в рабочих мозолях плывут и не ждут ничего.
Лимоны
и люди в Италии стоят дешевле всего.
Куда вы
спешите, все люди? Куда вы ползете, куда
удавы
брандспойтов, где буйно играет, как мышцы, вода?
Все — к Риму,
как будто бы к храму, где вам отпущенье дадут,
и к рынку,
где, может, вас купят, а может быть, и продадут.
Урвал бы
я опыта Рима, чтоб в жизни потом не пропасть.
Украл бы
чуть-чуть его ритма, — да нет, ни урвать,
ни украсть.

Есть Римы,
а Рима, наверное, просто физически нет.
Есть ритмы —
нет общего ритма, и в этом-то улиц секрет.
Но буду
старьевщиком лоскутов Рима, что порваны им.
Набухну,
как будто бы губка, всосавшая порами Рим.
До ночи
подслушивать стану, — и ночью, конечно, не спя,
доносчик
всему человечеству, Рим, на тебя и себя.
Напрячу
за пазуху все, что проулки твои накричат,
наплачут,
нашепчут, насвищут, налязгают и нажурчат.
Пусть гонка
за Римом по Риму мне кости ломает, дробя, —
как пленка,
я буду наматывать яростно Рим на себя ...

«Пожар! Пожар!
Горит синьора Сильвия!»
«Да нет,
дурак,
квартира —
не она ...»
«В шкафу
пошарь —
там есть белье носильное,
и тот
дуршлаг —
скорее из окна!
Кидай
диван
и крышку унитаза!
... а все — горбом,
ну хоть о стенку лбом ...
Постой, болван,
а где же наша ваза?
А где

альбом,
семейный наш альбом? ...»
«Заткнись,
жена,
тут не поможешь визгом ...»
«... Зачем
с греха
пошла я под венец?!»
«Веревку
на,
спускай-ка телевизор ...
Повешен —
ха! —
проклятый, наконец!»
«Не плачь,
все здесь —
кастрюли и бидоны.
Очнись,
жена,
смотри — ты вся в пуху ...»
«Отстань,
не лезь ...
Постой, а где мадонна?
Горит
она!
Забыли наверху!!»
«Беда,
беда ...
Ты слышал это, сын мой?»
«Теперь,
сосед,
для них потерян рай.
Теперь
всегда
страдать синьоре Сильвии ...
Мадонны нет ...
Забыли ... Ай-яй-яй! ...»

«Кому дуче,
кому дуче!

До чего хорош портрет!
Налетайте,
люди,
тучей, —
лучше парня в мире нет!
Кисть художника —
ну что ж! —
не матиссова,
но ведь вам когда-то вождь
нравился мольтиссимо.
Налетай,
блошиный рынок,
и торгуйся умненько.
Среди стольких птичек-рыбок
эта птичка —
уника!
Покупателей открытых
нет сегодня на вождя,
но с достатком шитых-крытых:
по глазам их вижу я.
Посмелей —
так будет лучше,
а то дуче трескается.
Кому дуче,
кому дуче!
Никому не требуется?»

«Сюда подходите, синьоры, —
здесь продаются письма.
Самые настоящие —
видите штемпеля?
Прошу не отклеивать марок —
читайте, не торопитесь . . .
Писем на всех достаточно —
целые штабеля.
Пожалуйста, век восемнадцатый:
« . . . Я буду вас ждать хоть вечность».
Пожалуйста, век девятнадцатый:
« . . . Я буду вас ждать хоть сто лет».
А вот и двадцатый, синьоры:

«... Чего ты все крутишь и вертишь?
Уже я потратил два вечера,
а результата нет».
Вот первая мировая,
а это уже вторая ...
(К несчастью, цензурные вымарки
временем не сняло ...)
А если третья случится —
синьоры, я представляю,
и вы представляете, думаю, —
не будет писем с нее.
Синьоры, по-моему, письма
дороже всяких реликвий,
но продают их дешево,
а я покупаю, старик.
Письма — странички разрозненные
книги, быть может, великой,
но нету такого клея,
чтоб склеить все вместе их».
«Синьор, вам не кажется странным,
что вы — продавец писем?»
«Странным? А что тут странного?
Ага, угадал — вы поэт ...
А вам не кажется странным,
что вы продавец песен?
В мире так много странного,
а в сущности, странного нет ...»

«Мама Рома, мама Рома,
как тебе не совестно?
Тощ супруг, как макарона,
да еще без соуса.
Меня совесть не грызет —
кровь грызет игривая.
Дай,
правительство,
развод,
или —
эмигрирую!»

— Синьор доктор, объясните мне, какое я
животное?
— Не понимаю вашего вопроса, синьора.
— Чего ж тут не понимать, синьор доктор!
Встаю и сразу начинаю штопать, гладить, готовить
завтрак мужу и детям — словом, верчусь, как
белка в колесе.

Сама поесть не успеваю — остаюсь голодная,
как волк.

Иду на фабрику и целый день ишачу.
Возвращаюсь в автобусе и шиплю на всех от злости,
как гусыня.

Захожу в магазин и тащусь оттуда, нагруженная,
как верблюд.

Прихожу домой и снова стираю, подметаю, готовлю, —
в общем, работаю как лошадь.
Падаю в кровать усталая, как собака.
Муж приходит пьяный, плюхается рядом и говорит:
«Подвинься, корова».

Какое же я все-таки животное, синьор доктор,
а синьор доктор?

«Исповедь кончается моя,
падре.
Нет волос, как прежде, у меня —
патлы.
Вы учили, падре, не грешить,
думать.
Я старалась, падре, так и жить —
дура.
Ничего не помню, как во сне.
Зряшно
так жила я праведно, что мне
страшно.
Согрешить бы перед смертью, но
поздно.
Лишь грехи, что были так давно,
помню.
Мне уже не надо ничего —
бабка.

Далеко до школьного того
банта.
Подойдите, что-то вам скажу,
внучки.
Истину, что крестик вам вложу
в ручки.
Вы не бойтесь, внученьки, грехов
нужных,
а вы бойтесь, внученьки, гробов
нудных.
Вы бегите дальше от пустой
веры
во грехи, как будто в лес густой,
вербный.
Вы услышьте, внученьки, тихи,
в стонах:
радость перед смертью — лишь грехи
вспомнить . . .»

«Счастливые билетики,
билетики,
билетики,
а в них мотоциклетики,
«фиатики»,
буфетики.
Не верьте ни политике,
ни дуре-кибернетике,
а верьте лишь в билетики,
счастливые билетики . . .
Сейчас на вас беретики,
а завтра вы — скелетики.
Хватайте же билетики,
счастливые билетики!»

«Если вы с неудач полысели,
то, синьоры, не будьте разинями —
вы купите себе полицейского
замечательного, резинового.

Бейте,
плюйте,
пинайте,

тычьте,
а когда его так поучите —
облегченье хотя бы частичное
в этой жизни треклятой получите . . .»
«А резиновых членов правительства,
вы скажите,
у вас не предвидится?»
«Обещать вам даже не пробую.
Сожалею, синьор, —
все проданы».
“Руки прочь,
руки прочь
от Вьетнама!
Бросим стирку нашу,
дочь,
как-никак,
я мама.
Ну зачто они бомбят
Тех детишек —
вьетнамят,
или все бездетны,
или врут газеты?”

А я — плевал я на Вьетнам!
Мне бы — тихо жить.
Мне —
заплатку бы к штанам
новую пришить!»
«Синьор сержант,
синьор сержант,
у Пьяцца ди Эспанья
искала я себе сервант
и секретер для спальни.
И вдруг — витрина,
в ней кровать,
а на кровати девка,
в чем родила, конечно, мать,
лежит и курит дерзко.
А рядом с девкою лежат
кальсоны чьи-то сальные

и сверх того,
синьор сержант,
пустые ...
эти самые.
А над стыдобищем таким
написано:
«Скульптура».
Синьор сержант,
спасите Рим
и римскую культуру!»
«Рим спасти, синьора, сложно ...
Что поделать —
молодежь ...
А что можно,
что не можно —
в наши дни не разберешь ...»

«Стриптиз, наоборот,
сейчас у нас в новиночках».
«Что это за штуковина?»
«А делается так:
выходит, значит, дамочка —
лишь бляшечки на титечках,
а после одевается,
и в этом — самый смак».
«Старо ...
На сцену жизни
все выползают голыми,
а после одеваются
в слова,
слова,
слова,
но под словами все-таки
друг друга видят голыми.
Стриптиз наоборот — ля вита такова ...»
— Синьор, я хозяин бара, и, конечно, это не мое дело; но я хотел бы предупредить вас, что женщина, подсевшая к вашему столику, — извиняюсь, мужчина ...
— Что за странная шутка!
— К сожалению, это не шутка, а жизненный опыт, синьор. Обратите внимание на руки и ноги — они чересчур крупные и мускулистые. Расти-

тельность снята с лица снециальной пастой. Длинные волосы — или парик, или свои, отпущенные. Вас, может быть, ввела в заблуждение выпуклая форма груди? Это следствие парафиновых инъекций. Болезненно, но действенно. Синьор, вы еще очень молоды и, видимо, неопытны, поэтому я счел своим долгом несколько неделикатно предупредить вас ...
— Значит, эта женщина — мужчина?
— Мужчина, синьор ...
— Черт знает что такое! Кстати, называйте меня не синьор, а синьорина. Я уже столько дней безрезультатно ищу себе хоть одну настоящую женщину ... Что поделаешь — не везет ...

«Синьоры!
От имени и по поручению президиума Клуба педерастов разрешите мне поднять первый тост за женщин. Пусть вас не удивляет этот тост, синьоры. При всех их физических и моральных недостатках женщины необходимы для того, чтобы рождать нас, педерастов. Итак — за женщин!»

«Мой друг, скажи, к чему писать стихи
среди распада страшного? Не знаю.
Как этот мир сурово ни стыди,
не устыдится. Предан стыд, как знамя.

Спасение в стыде, но он забыт,
и мне порою хочется воскликнуть:
«О, где же, человечество, твой стыд —
единственный твой двигатель великий?

Вокруг бесстыдство царствует в ночи,
а чувства и мельчают и увечатся, —
лишь пьяниц жилковатые носы
краснеют от стыда за человечество ...»

«Постой, постой ... Твой горький монолог
уже стихи ... Писать их, значит, стоит.
А не захочешь — так заставит бог,
который в нас, несовершенных, стонет.

Да, стыд забыт, — вернее, он притих,
но только сокрушаться не годится.
Ведь ты стыдишься! Почему в других
потеряна способность устыдиться?!

Бездейственно следить чужой разврат —
не лучше откровенного разврата,
и, проклиная свысока распад,
мы сами — составная часть распада.

Ну, а тебе не кажется, мой друг,
что, зренье потерявши от испуга,
мы в замкнутый с тобой попали круг,
не видя мира за чертою круга?

Но есть совсем другие круги, есть
и в этот миг — нетронуто, старинно, —
любовь, надежда, доброта и честь
идут, для нас незримые, по Риму.

Они для нас, как мы для них, — в тени.
Они идут. Как призраков, нас гонят.
И может, правы именно они
и вечны, словно Вечный этот город».

«Забыли нас, любимый мой.
Из парка все ушли домой,
и с чертового колеса
стекли куда-то голоса.

Механик, видно, добрый был —
на землю нас не опустил.
Остановилось колесо.
Забыли нас ... Как хорошо!

Внизу наш бедный гордый Рим,
любимый Рим, проклятый Рим.
Не знает он, что мы над ним
в своей кабиночке парим.

Внизу политики-врали,
министры, шлюхи, короли,
чины, полиция, войска —
какая это все тоска!

Кому-то мы внизу нужны,
и что-то делать мы должны.
Спасибо им, что хоть сейчас
на небесах забыли нас.

Чуть-чуть кабиночку качни
и целовать меня начни,
не то сама ее качну
и целовать тебя начну».

Постой, война, постой, война . . .
Да, жизнь, как Рим, — она страшна,
но жизнь, как Рим, она — одна . . .
Постой, война, постой, война . . .

[*Литературная газета,* 1965]

ПРОЦЕССИЯ С МАДОННОЙ

Людовико Коррао

В городишке тихом Таормина
стройно шла процессия с мадонной.
Дым свечей всходил и таял мирно,
невесомый, словно тайна мига.

Впереди, шли девочки — все в белом
и держали свечи крепко-крепко.
Шли они с восторгом оробелым,
полные собой и миром целым.

И глядели девочки на свечи
и в неверном пламени дрожащем
видели загадочные встречи,
слышали заманчивые речи.

Девочкам надеяться пристало.
Время обмануться не настало,
но, как будто их судьба, за ними
позади шли женщины устало.

Позади шли женщины — все в черном
и держали свечи тоже крепко.
Шли тяжелым шагом удрученным,
полные обманом уличенным.

И глядели женщины на свечи
и в неверном пламени дрожащем
видели детей худые плечи,
слышали мужей тупые речи.

Шли все вместе, улицы минуя,
матерью мадонну именуя,
и несли мадонну на носилках,
будто бы стоячую больную.

И мадонна, видимо, болела
равно и за девочек и женщин,
но мадонна, видимо, велела,
чтобы был такой порядок вечен.

Я смотрел, идя с мадонной рядом,
ни светло, ни горестно на свечи,
а каким-то двуединым взглядом,
полным и надеждою и ядом.

Так вот и живу — необрученным
и уже навеки обреченным
где-то между девочками в белом
и седыми женщинами в черном.

Сицилия [*Юность*, 1966]

У РИМСКОЙ ЗАБЫТОЙ ДОРОГИ

У римской забытой дороги
недалеко от Дамаска
мертвенны гор отроги,
как императоров маски.

Кольца на солнце грея,
сдержанно скрытноваты,
нежатся жирные змеи —
только что с Клеопатры.

Везли по дороге рубины,
мечи из дамасской стали,
и волосами рабыни,
корчась, ее подметали.

В язвах богини Венеры,
панцирями одетых,
шагали легионеры
с лицами, как на монетах.

Еще не ставшие щебнем,
покачивались колесницы,
подобные гнутым гребням
в прическе императрицы.

Плиты дороги были
крепко рабами сбиты,
будто в дорогу вбили
окаменевшие спины.

Изнемогая от солнца,
мазью натершись этрусской,
с чашей лимонного сока
мыслил патриций обрюзглый:

«Пусть от рабочей черни
лишь черепа да ребра,
мы не умрем, как черви,
и не умрет дорога . . .»

И мыслил араб-строитель,
покорно бивший кувалдой,

но все-таки раб строптивый,
но все-таки раб коварный:

«Думая лишь о плоти,
вы позабыли бога.
Значит, и вы умрете,
значит, умрет и дорога . . .»

Сгнивали империи корни.
Она, расползаясь, зияла,
как сшитое нитками крови
лоскутное одеяло.

Опять применяли опыт
улещиванья и пыток,
кровью пытались штопать,
но нет ненадежней ниток!

С римского лицемерия
спала надменная тога,
и умерла империя,
и умерла дорога.

Пытались прибегнуть к подлогу.
Твердили, что в крови, когда-то
пролитой на дорогу,
дорога не виновата.

Но дикой травы поколенья
с ней счеты сводили крупно.
Родившая преступленья,
дорога — сама преступна.

И всем палачам-дорогам
и всем дорогам-тиранам
да будет высоким итогом —
высокая плата бурьяном!

Так думал я на дороге,
теперь для проезда закрытой,
дороге, забывшей о боге
и богом за это забытой.

Дамаск-Москва, 1967–1968

[*Огонек,* 1968]

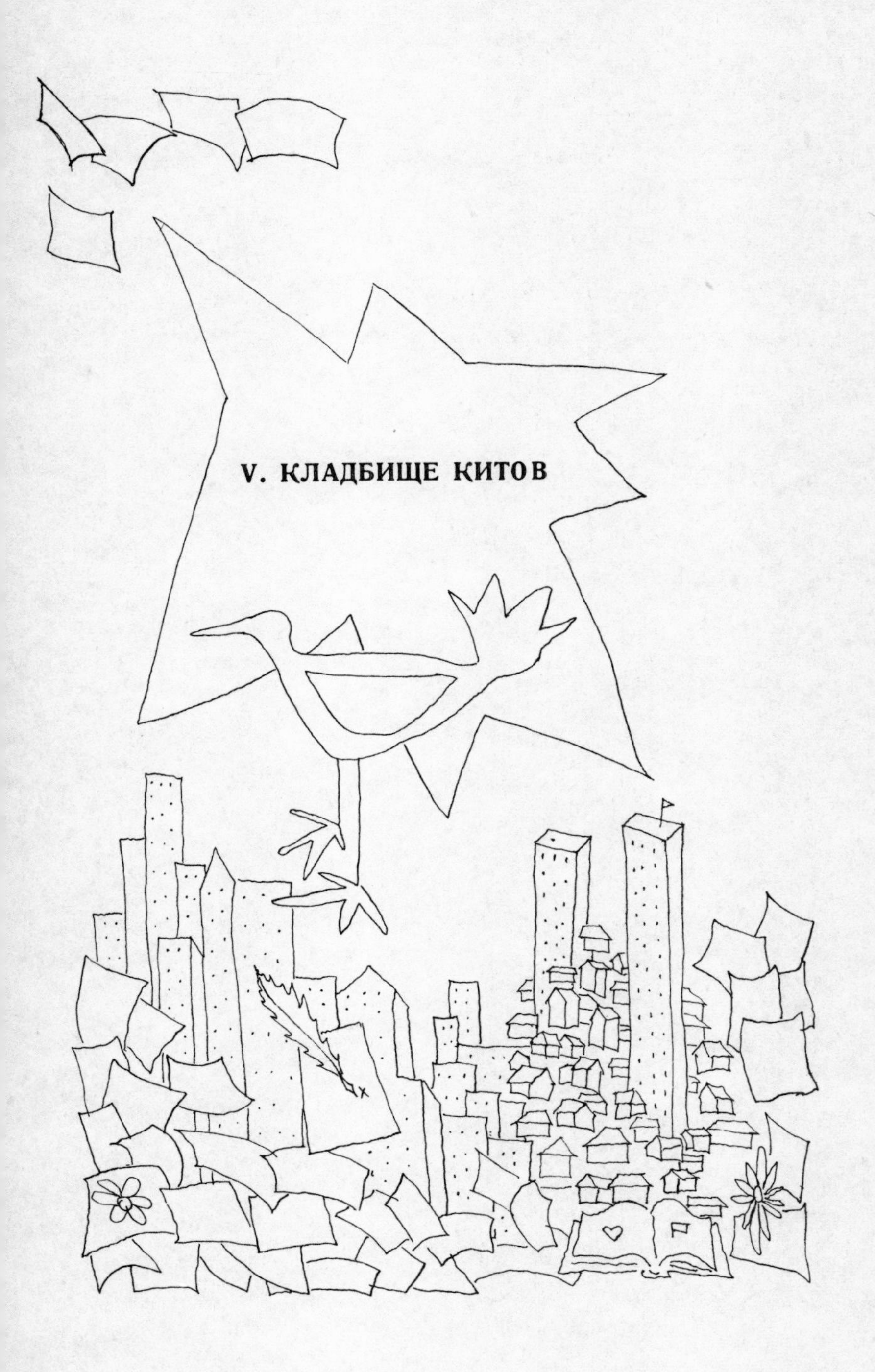

V. КЛАДБИЩЕ КИТОВ

В ДОМЕ СТАЛЕВАРА

Люблю Америку,
которая плыла
по майской Эльбе,
поднимая виски
в усталой правой,
подгребая левой,
ну а навстречу ей плыла Россия
по майской Эльбе,
поднимая водку
в усталой левой,
подгребая правой,
и водка с виски —
без! без перевода
так понимали —
чорт возьми! —
друг друга
над вспененой водой победы обшей!

Люблю Америку,
которая сейчас
сидит со мной в коттеджике стандартном
сталелитейщика,
и на руках рабочих
натруженные жилы проступают,
как тайные притоки нашей Эльбы,
и между нами нет сейчас правительств.
Правительство невидимое наше
сейчас безмолвно выбранное нами, —
те самые усталые солдаты
ребята из Иркутска и Кентукки
которые невидимо к друг другу
по майской Эльбе до сих пор плывут.
Шумят,
шумят невидимые волны
по братскому непышному столу,
и нами рюмки с плохоньким портвейном
качаются чуть-чуть на этих волнах,
алея, словно бакены надежды.

Мы говорим,
как будто мы плывем
чтобы обняться, словно братья,
но
за двадцать лет так засорили Эльбу!
В нее спустили столько нечистот
заводы лжи —
суперклоаки века.
Газеты, все пропитанные ядом,
окурки поджигательских речей,
плевки мерзавцев,
грязный «kleenex» мятый,
брезгливо вытиравший жирный пот
с фальшивых лиц ораторов заядлых . . .
А под водою нашей Эльбы скрыты
замшелейшие мины недоверья,
и новенькие гладкие подлодки,
брюхатые торпедами, как будто
детьми от брака страха
и науки . . .
Ккогда,
когда друг друга мы поймем
как водка с виски —
без! без перевода
так понимали —
чорт возьми! —
друг друга
над вспененной водой победы общей?
Неужто нужен новый Гитлер нам
чтоб мы объединились,
как когда-то?
Цена —
похоже —
слишком дорогая . . .
Россия и Америка,
ваш путь
к друг другу сложен,
но я верю,
верю
что через все отбросы или мины

мы доплывем к друг другу,
доплывем,
и мы обнимемся,
как в мае, в сорок пятом,
на этот раз —
я верю —
навсегда!

Да,
между нами океаны злобы,
Да,
между нами океан Великий,
но поплывем,
и превратитеся в Эльбу
любой великий самый океан!
. . . Люблю Америку,
которая сейчас
ножонками болтает в колыбельке,
светящими усталым грустным нам,
как тоненькие свечечки надежды.
Как ее имя —
Джен?
А, может, Лара?

Ее глаза,
большие,
голубые,
как будто две доверчивые капли
той самой Эльбы,
нашей обшей Эльбы,
которую не вправе мы предать.
. . . Россия и Америка,
плывите!

[*Литературная газета,* 1966]

МОНОЛОГ БРОДВЕЙСКОЙ АКТРИСЫ

Сказала актриса с Бродвея
разрушенно, будто бы древняя Троя:
«Нет роли!
Нет роли такой,
чтоб всю душу мне вывернуть!
Нет роли такой,
чтоб все слезы мне выреветь!
От жизни такой
хоть беги в чисто поле ...
Нет роли!
Как шапка на воре пылает Бродвей ...
Нет роли,
нет роли
средь сотен ролей.
Мы тонем в безролье ...
Где взять гениальных писателей!
А классики взмокли,
как будто команда спасателей.
Но что они знали
про Хиросиму,
про гибель безвинных,
про все наши боли?
Неужто все это невыразимо?
Нет роли.
Без роли —
как будто без компаса.
Ты знаешь, как страшен свет,
когда в тебе копится,
копится,
а выхода этому нет.
Пожалте, гастроли,
пожалте, уют.
Отобраны роли.
Ролишки суют.
Я пью ...
Понимаю, конечно, что это безвольно.
Но что же поделать,

когда так безлюдно, безрольно!
Пьет где-то рабочий
и грани стакана в нигроле . . .
Нет роли!
Пьет фермер,
мыча от сознанья бессилья и боли . . .
Нет роли!
Парнишку шестнадцати лет от безделья дружки
финкарем пропороли . . .
Нет роли!
Молчавший о зверских убийствах,
истошно вопит на судью,
но где? —
на футболе . . .
Нет роли!
Без роли вся жизнь — это тление.
Мы все гениальны в утробе,
но гибнут возможные гении
при невозможности роли.
Не требуя чьей-нибудь крови —
я
требую
роли!»

1967

[*Знамя*, 1967]

К ВОПРОСУ О СВОБОДЕ

Зола Дахау жжет мне до сих пор подметки.
Дымятся подо мной асфальт или паркет.
Как гвозди палачей, мне всажены под ногти
неправые штыки и острия ракет.

Поглажу я рукой любимой сонный локон,
а сам курю, курю, и это неспроста.
Я распят, как Христос, на крыльях самолетов,
летящих в эту ночь бомбить детей Христа.

Бросает кожу в дрожь от взрывов и от рева,
как будто бы она-вьетнамская земля,
и, хрупая хребтом, разламывая ребра,
берлинская стена проходит сквозь меня.

Вы о свободе мне? Досужее позерство
под сенью роковой, висящих в небе бомб.
От века своего свободным быть позорно.
Позорней во сто крат, чем быть его рабом.

Да, несвободен я и от ташкентских женщин,
и от далласких пуль, и от пекинских фраз,
и от вьетнамских вдов, и от российских женщин
с кайлами возле рельс, в платочках ниже глаз!

Да, несвободен я от Пушкина и Блока,
от штата Мэриленд и станции Зима.
Да, несвободен я от дьявола и бога,
от красоты земли и от ее дерьма.

Да, несвободен я от жажды мокрой шваброй
пройтись по головам среди грызни, резни.
Да, несвободен я от чести в морду шваркнуть
всем в мире сволочам, что сволочи они!

И, может буду тем любезен я народу,
что прожил жизнь, борясь, — не попросту скорбя,
что в мой жестокий век восславил несвободу
от праведной борьбы, свобода, за тебя ...

[*Литературная газета*, 1966]

РЕСТОРАН ДЛЯ ДВОИХ

Гонолулу,
на спине ты качаешься сонно в серебряно-черном нигде.
Гонит луны
вдоль зазывно-русалочьих бедер твоих ветерок по воде.
Всюду блестки.
По-дикарски ты любишь стекляшки витрин и реклам.
Словно брошки,
пароходы приколоты к влажным твоим волосам.
Ты тасуешь
австралийцев, японцев и янки в шальных шоколадных руках.
Ты танцуешь,
и звенят золоченые рыбки в стеклянных твоих каблучках.
Лорд-шотландец
в пестрой юбочке пляшет с тобою, пуская слюну,
и, шатаясь,
лезет мокро под юбку, и, кажется, не под свою.
Но, как гномик,
дотянулся до звезд на ходулях — на пальмовых сваях своих
крошка-домик,
уникальный игрушечный храм — ресторан для двоих.
Без антенны
его крыша из листьев — зеленый смешной колпачок.
Его стены
из бамбука и тайны, а что там творится — молчок!
Бой-малаец
на подносе эбеновом вносит по лестнице в дом,
ухмыляясь,
запеченный акулий плавник в ананасе насквозь золотом.
Два прибора.
Две свечи. Два лица. Два сообщника. Два беглеца.
Как в соборы,
от содома они убежали к друг другу в глаза.
Ненадежно,
как в фонарике елочном здесь, и, пожалуй, морально грешно.
В общем, ложно,
в общем, призрачно это, а все-таки так хорошо!
Трепет самбы,
лепет звезд и раскаты прибоя у дамбы — все только для них!

Я и сам бы
драпанул с удовольствием в тот ресторан для двоих!
Подлым харям
закричал бы я, в пальцах обрыдлый бокал раздавив:
«По-ды-хаю
от тоски среди вас. Я хочу в ресторан для двоих!»
Надо делать
то и это, а этого — ни при каких?
На-до-ело!
Я смертельно устал. Я хочу в ресторан для двоих.
Надо думать
и бороться за что-то? Пытался я. Пробовал. Фиг!
Надоумил
этот домик меня. Я хочу в ресторан для двоих!
Пусть осудят —
удеру! Но бежать — это только для трусов, трусих.
Что же будет,
если каждый запрячется в свой ресторан для двоих?!!
Среди гнойных
всех нарывов эпохи не выход — бежать от тоски
в домик-гномик,
в чьи-то волосы, губы, колени, ладони, виски!
Шепот беса
нас толкает к побегам, а мы не умеем понять:
после бегства
пострашней оказаться на каторге прежней опять.
. . . В звездных безднах,
будто в хрупком кораблике, тихо сидят, нашалив,
двое беглых,
а внизу ожидает с овчарками жизнь, как шериф.
И малаец
на приступочке дремлет внизу — на заветной черте,
умиляясь
так презрительно чьей-то святой и пустой простоте.
Замечает,
что еще полчаса до закрытья, а после — катись! —
и включает
для иллюзии рая — на пленку записанных птиц . . .

1967

[*Литературная газета*, 1967]

БАЛЛАДА О САМОРОДКАХ

Ночной Фербанкс притих, устав,
но всюду скрыты
по снежным улицам в унтах
гуляют скрипы.
В оленьей парке расписной
с лицом подростка
спешит работать в бар ночной
стрип-эскимоска.
Бухие летчики-дружки
с военной базы
швыряют в спину ей снежки,
томясь без бабы.
Ну а она несет впотьмах,
сквозь морды, хари,
как розу белую в зубах,
свое дыханье.

С морозу в двери кабака,
седы, как луни,
заходят шумно облака.
Внутри их — люди.
Охотники, и скорняки,
и парни с шахты
все на моржовые клыки
скидают шапки.
Кто представляет чей-то флаг?
Здесь не до флага.
Среди аляскинских бродяг
я свой, бродяга.
И нам превыше всяких благ
святая влага!
Ты пьешь со мною, старый Боб,
мой новый кореш.
Меня ручищами ты сгреб,
щетиной колешь.
Сверкает золотом оскал.

Ты худ и страшен.
«Всю жизнь я золото искал — ты слышишь? —
рашен!
Я был румяный — будь здоров! —
теперь я черен.
Аэродром для комаров —
мой лысый череп.
Я подвожу теперь черту —
остался рванью.
Сплошное золото во рту,
и медь в кармане.
У мерзлой ямы на краю
собаки выли,
когда я хоронил свою
старуху Виви.
Была девчонка первый класс, —
как на картинках!
Все тело белое, что кварц, —
чуть в золотинках.
Я молодой, глазастый был —
не из несчастных.
Сказал: «Тебя я застолбил.
Ты — мой участок».
Я мучил Виви сорок лет.
Я сумасбродно
всю жизнь хотел напасть на след —
на самородки!
Она хотела не тряпья,
а сына робко.
Ей снился сын такой, как я,
мне — самородки.
Я пил.
Но плыли на меня
из мутной водки,
как рыбы желтые, дразня,
те самородки.
И я закрыл свой личный трест,
банкрот хрипатый.
Я сколотил для Виви крест —
кирку с лопатой.

Я вез тот гроб — я не забыл! —
на санках мерзлых.
Я не отрыл,
а я зарыл
мой самородок ...»
Сгребает центы Боб в горсти.
Он пьян и мрачен.
«Без самородков я — прости.
Поставь мне, рашен!»
Он открывает дверь пинком,
забыв про шапку,
ныряет в облако, и в нем
уходит шатко.
И я, как он, иду во тьме,
дитя шалмана,
и не оттягивает мне
ничто кармана.
Свой трест еще я не закрыл —
я слишком робок,
но может быть, уже зарыл
свой самородок.
И рядом спутницей немой
с лицом подростка
бредет измученно домой
стрип-эскимоска.
Мороз. Сосульки у меня
на подбородке,
и звезды падают, звеня,
как самородки ...

1967

[*Правда,* 1967]

КЛАДБИЩЕ КИТОВ

На кладбище китов
на снеговом погосте
стоят взамен крестов
их собственные кости.
Они не по зубам —
все зубы мягковаты.
Они не по супам —
кастрюли мелковаты.
Их вьюга, тужась, гнет,
но держатся-порядок! —
вколоченные в лед,
как дуги черных радуг.
Горбатый эскимос,
тоскующий о стопке,
как будто бы вопрос,
в них заключен, как в скобки.
Кто резво щелкнул там?
Ваш фотопыл умерьте!
Дадим покой китам
хотя бы после смерти.
. . . А жили те киты,
людей не обижая,
от десткой простоты
фонтаны обожая.
И солнца красный шар
плясал на струях белых . . .
«Киты по борту! Жарь!
Давай, ребята, бей их!»
Спастись куда-нибудь?
Но ты-пространства шире.
А под воду нырнуть —
воды нехватит в мире.
Ты думаешь, ты бог?
Рисковая нескромность.
Гарпун получишь в бок
расплатой за огромность.
Огромность всем велит
охотиться за нею.

Тот дурень, кто велик.
Кто мельче-тот умнее.
Плотва, как вермишель.
Среди ее безличья
дразнящая мишень
беспомощность величья.
Бинокли на борту
в руках дрожат, нацелясь,
и с гарпуном в боку
Толстой бежит от «цейсов».
Китеныш, а не кит,
но, словно кит оценен,
гарпунным тросом взвит,
качается Есенин.
Кровав китовый сан.
Величье убивает.
И Маяковский сам
гарпун в себя вбивает.
Величью мель страшна.
На камни брошен гонкой,
обломки гарпуна
выхаркивает Горький.
Почти не простонав,
по крови, как по следу,
уходит Пастернак
с обрывком троса —
в Лету.
Хемингуей молчит,
но над могилой грозно
гарпун в траве торчит
проросший ввысь из гроба.
И, скрытый за толпой,
кровавым занят делом
даллаский китобой
с оптическим прицелом.
. . . Идет большой загон,
а после смерти-ласка.
Честнее твой закон,
жестокая Аляска.
На кладбище китов

у ледяных торосов
нет ханжеских цветов —
есть такт у эскимосов.
Эх, эскимос-горбун, —
у белых свой обычай:
сперва всадив гарпун,
поплакать над добычей.
Скорбят смиренней дев,
сосут в слезах пилюли
убийцы, креп надев,
в почетном карауле.
И промысловики,
которым здесь не место,
несут китам венки
от Главгарпунотреста.
Но скручены цветы
стальным гарпунным тросом.
Довольно доброты!
Пустите к эскимосам!

1967

[*Москва*, 1967]

НЬЮ-ЙОРКСКАЯ ЭЛЕГИЯ

В центральном парке города Нью-Йорка
Среди ночей, продрогнувший, ничей
я говорил с Америкой негромко —
мы оба с ней устали от речей.

Я говорил с Америкой шагами,
а зто не слова — они не врут,
и отвечала мне она кругами
от мертвых листьев, падающих в пруд.

Шел снег. Себя он чувствовал неловко
у баров, продолжеющих гульбу,
садясь на жилы вспухшие неона

у города бессонного на лбу,
на бодрую улыбку кандидата,
пытавшегося влезть не без труда
куда не помню — помню, что куда-то,
но снегу было все равно куда.

А в парке здесь он надал бестревожно,
и как на разноцветные плоты
снежинки опускались осторожно
на тонущие медленно листы,
на шар воздушный, розовый и зыбкий,
о звезды сонно трущийся щекой,
прилепленный жевательной резинкой
к стволу сосны ребяческой рукой,
на чью-то позабытую перчатку,
на зоосад, спровадивший гостей
и на скамейку с надписью печальной:
«Здесь место для потерянных детей».

Олени снег потерянно лизали.
Мерцали белки у чугунных ваз
среди дерев потерянных лесами,
потерянными бусинками глаз

Храня в себе сурово и сокрыто
безмолвно вопрошающий укор
лежали глыбы грузные гранита —
потерянные дети бывших гор.

Жевали зебры за решеткой сено,
потерянно уставясь в темноту.
Моржи, вздымая морды из бассейна,
ловили снег усами на лету.

Моржи глядели горько и туманно,
по-своему жалея, как могли,
потерянные дети океана,
людей — детей потерянных земли.

Я шел один, и лишь вдали за чащей
как будто ночи пристальный зрачок,
перед лицом невидимым парящий
плыл сигареты красный светлячок,

и чудилось — искала угловато,
не зная, что об этом я молю,
потерянность неведомая чья-то
потерянность похожую мою.

И под бесшумным белым снегопадом,
объединявшим тайною своей,
Америка со мной садилась рядом
на место для потерянных детей.

[*Знамя*, 1967]

МОНОЛОГ АМЕРИКАНСКОГО ПОЭТА

Роберту Лоуэллу

Уходит любимая,
будто бы воздух из легких,
навек растворяясь в последних снежинках излетных
в качанье ветвей с почернелою провисью льдышек ...
Обратно не вдышишь!
Напрасно щекою я трусь о шершавый понуренный хобот
трубы водосточной ...
Напрасно я плачу —
уходит.
Уходят друзья,
кореша,
однолетки,
как будто с площадки молодняка
нас кто-то разводит в отдельные клетки
от некогда общего молока.
Напрасно скулю по друзьям,
как звереныш ...

Друзей не воротишь!
Уходят надежды —
такие прекрасные дамы,
которых я выбрал в такие напрасные даты.
В руках остается лишь край их одежды,
но жалкое знамя —
клочок от надежды ...
Уходит уверенность ...
Помнится —
клялся я страшной божбою
о стену башку проломить
или стену — башкою.
Башка поцарапана, правда, но, в общем, цела,
а что со стеной?
Ухмыляется, сволочь-стена, —
лишь дворник на ней равнодушно меняет портреты ...
Уверенность,
где ты?
Я словно корабль,
на котором все гибелью пахнет,
и прыгают крысы ослизлые в панике с палуб.
Эй, чайки!
Не надо Не плачьте —
жалеть меня бросьте.
Меня покидают мои длинноногие гостьи.
Садятся они, как положено, первыми в лодки ...
Прощайте, красотки!
Меня покидают мои краснощекие юнги.
Им хочется жить.
Справедливо.
Они еще юны.
Прощайте, мальчишки!
Гребите вперед.
Вы мужчины.
А я выключаю бессмысленный рокот машины,
и только талант
капитаном небритым и пьяным
на мостике мрачно стоит
капитан капитаном.

Но, грязные слезы размазав по грубой обветренной
коже,
он тоже меня покидает.
Он тоже, он тоже ...
Эй, шлюпки,
а ну от греха отойдите в сторонку!
Корабль, если тонет,
вокруг образует воронку.
Остаться совсем одному —
это боль ножевая,
но втягивать я за собой никого не желаю.
Я всех вас прощаю,
одетый в предсмертную пену,
а вам завещаю
пробить ту проклятую стену
и вас призываю
торчащей в завертинах белых трубою
к бою ...

1967 [*Знамя,* 1967]

МОНОЛОГ ПЕСЦА НА АЛЯСКИНСКОЙ ЗВЕРОФЕРМЕ

Я голубой на звероферме серой,
но, цветом обреченный на убой,
за непрогрызной проволочной сеткой
не утешаюсь тем, что голубой.

И я бросаюсь в линьку, я лютую,
себя сдираю яростно с себя,
но голубое, брызжа и ликуя,
сквозь шкуру прет, предательски слепя.

И вою я, ознобно, тонко вою
трубой косматой страшного суда,
прося у звезд или навеки волю,
или хотя бы линьку навсегда.

Заезжий мистер на магнитофоне
запечатлел мой вой. Какой простак!
Он просто сам не выл, а мог бы тоже
завыть, сюда попав, еще не так!

И падаю на пол, подыхаю
и все никак подохнуть не могу.
Гляжу с тоской на мой родной Дахау
и знаю: никогда не убегу.

Однажды, тухлой рыбой пообедав,
увидел я, что дверь не на крючке,
и прыгнул в бездну звездную побега
с бездумностью, обычной в новичке.

Вокруг Аляска высилась сугробно,
а я скакал, отчаянный, чумной,
и в легких танцевала твист свобода,
со звездами глотаемая мной.

Я куролесил. Я точил балясы
с деревьями. Я был самим собой.
И снег, переливаясь, не боялся
того, что он такой же голубой.

Мать и отец друг друга не любили,
а спаривались Как бы я хотел
найти подругу, чтобы в снежной пыли
я с нею кувыркался и летел!

Но я устал. Меня сбивали вьюги.
Я вытащить не мог завязших лап.
И не было ни друга, ни подруги.
Дитя неволи для свободы слаб.

Кто в клетке зачат, тот по клетке плачет.
И с ужасом я понял, что люблю
ту клетку, где меня за сетку прячут,
и звероферму — родину мою.

И я вернулся, жалкий и побитый,
но только оказался в клетке вновь,
как виноватость сделалась обидой
и превратилась в ненависть любовь.

Потерянно я выл в тебе, Аляска.
Потерянно я выл теперь в тюрьме.
Америка моя, я потерялся,
но кто не потерявшийся в тебе?

На звероферме, правда, перемены.
Душили раньше попросту в мешках.
Теперь нас убивают современно —
электротоком. Чисто как-никак!

Гляжу на эскимоску-звероводку.
По мне шуршит ласкательно рука,
и чешут пальцы мой загривок кротко,
но в ангельских глазах ее тоска.

Она меня спасет от всех болезней
и помереть мне с голоду не даст,
но знаю, что меня в мой срок железный,
как это ей положено, предаст.

Она воткнет, пролив из глаз водицу,
мне провод в рот, обманчиво шепча . . .
Гуманны будьте к служащим! Введите
на зверофермах должность палача!

Хотел бы я наивным быть, как предок,
но я рожден в неволе, я не тот.
Кто меня кормит, тем я буду предан.
Кто меня гладит, тот меня убьет.

[*Знамя*, 1967]

ЦВЕТЫ И ПУЛИ

Тот, кто любит цветы,
тот, естественно, пулям не нравится.
Пули — леди ревнивые.
Стоит ли ждать доброты!
Девятнадцатилетняя Аллисон Краузе,
ты убита за то,
что любила цветы.
Это было —
чистейших надежд выражение
в миг,
когда, беззащитна, как совести тоненький пульс,
ты вложила цветок
в держимордово дуло ружейное
и сказала:
«Цветы лучше пуль».
Не дарите цветов государству,
где правда карается.
Государства такого отдарок циничен,
жесток,
и отдарком была тебе,
Аллисон Краузе,
пуля,
вытолкнувшая цветок.
Пусть все яблони мира
не в белое —
в траур оденутся!
Ах, как пахнет сирень,
но не чувствуешь ты ничего.
Как сказал президент про тебя,
ты «бездельница».
Каждый мертвый — бездельник,
но это — вина не его.
Ты лежишь на траве
с карамелькой, запрятанной за щеку.
Новых платьев тебе не надеть,
новых книг не прочесть.
Ты студенткой была.
Изучала искусства изящные,

но другое искусство —
кровавое, страшное есть.
В том искусстве палаческом тоже, наверно,
есть гении.
Кто был Гитлер?
Новаторских газовых камер кубист.
От лица всех цветов
проклинаю я ваши творения,
архитекторы лжи,
дирижеры убийств!
Шепчут матери мира:
«О боже, о боже . . .»
И гадалки боятся
загадывать наперед.
Рок-н-ролл на костях
смерть танцует сейчас во Вьетнаме,
Камбодже,
и какую эстраду
она себе завтра найдет?!
Встаньте, девочки Токио,
мальчики Рима,
поднимайте цветы
против общего злого врага.
Дуньте разом на все одуванчики мира —
о, какая великая будет пурга!
Собирайтесь, цветы, на войну!
Покарайте карателей!
За тюльпаном тюльпан,
за левкоем — левкой,
вырываясь от гнева
из клумб аккуратненьких,
глотки всех лицемеров
заткните корнями с землей!
Ты опутай, жасмин,
миноносцев подводные лопасти!
Залепляя прицелы,
ты в линзы отчаянно впейся, репей!
Встаньте, лилии Ганга
и нильские лотосы,
и скрутите винты самолетов,

беременных смертью детей!
Розы, вы не гордитесь, когда продадут
подороже!
Пусть приятно касаться девической нежной
щеки, —
бензобаки
прокалывая
бомбардировщикам,
подлинней,
поострей отрастите шипы!
Если даже цветы восстают,
то негоже играться с историей в прятки.
Молодая Америка,
руки убийцам свяжи!
Нарастай,
нарастай,
эскалация правды,
против топчущей жизни людей
эскалации лжи!
Собирайтесь, цветы, на войну!
Защитите прекрасное!
Затопите шоссе и проселки,
как армии грозный поток,
и в колонны людей и цветов
встань, убитая Аллисон Краузе,
как бессмертник эпохи —
протеста колючий цветок!

1970

[*Правда*, 1970]

СВОБОДА УБИВАТЬ

Цвет статуи Свободы —
он все мертвенней
когда, свободу пулями любя,
сама в себя стреляешь ты,
Америка.
Ты можешь так совсем убить себя!
Опасно выйти
в мире этом дьявольском,
еще опасней —
прятаться в кустах,
и пахнет на земле всемирным
Далласом,
и страшно жить,
и стыден этот страх.
Кто станет верить в сказку лицемерную,
когда под сенью благостных идей
растет цена на смазку револьверную
и падает цена на жизнь людей?!
Убийцы ходят в трауре на похороны,
а после входят в дельце на паях,
и вновь
колосья, пулями наполненные,
качаются в Техасе на полях.
Глаза убийц под шляпами и кепками,
шаги убийц слышны у всех дверей,
и падает уже второй из Кеннеди ...
Америка, спаси своих детей!
Когда с ума опасно сходит нация,
то от беды ее не исцелит
спокойствие,
прописанное наскоро.
Ей, может быть, одно поможет —
стыд.
Историю не выстираешь в прачечной.
Еще таких машин стиральных нет.
Не сходит вечно кровь!
О, где он прячется,
стыд нации,

как будто беглый негр?!
Рабы — в рабах.
Полно убийц раскованных.
Они вершат свой самосуд,
погром,
и бродит по Америке Раскольников,
сойдя с ума,
с кровавым топором.
Эй, старый Эйби,
что же люди делают,
усвоив подло истину одну,
что только по поваленному дереву
легко понять его величину.
Линкольн хрипит в гранитном кресле ранено.
В него стреляют вновь!
Зверье — зверьем.
И звезды,
словно пуль прострелы рваные,
Америка,
на знамени твоем!
Восстань из мертвых,
столько раз убитая,
заговори,
как женщина и мать,
восстань,
Свободы статуя пробитая,
и прокляни свободу убивать!
Но к небу,
воззывая о растоптанности,
не отерев кровавых брызг с чела,
свое лицо зеленое утопленницы
ты,
статуя Свободы,
подняла . . .

1968

[*Правда*, 1968]

СМОГ

Я просыпаюсь в гостинице «Челси».
Чудится мне
(Это бред?
Это жар?) —
черные струйки,
как черные черви,
в щели вползают на всех этажах.
Галя в рубашке ночной, словно в саване.
Кашель ей грудь раздирает,
как рашпиль.
А на рубашке,
как уголь на сахаре,
черная копоть . . .
«Женя, мне страшно . . .»
В комнате-камере
запах Дахау.
«Женечка, милый,
я задыхаюсь . . .»
Лик ее мученический,
как из воска.
«Воздуха,
воздуха . . .»
Настежь окно,
но уже мне не чудится —
в комнату лезет косматое чудище,
движется облаком, черным, зыбучим . . .
«Женя,
задушит! . . .»
Галя,
я сам уже полузадушен.
Воздух глотаю,
но он безвоздушен.
Нету отдушин!
В губыкдруг другу отчаянно рухнем?
Будем дышать, как спасеньем, друг другом?
Но не уйти от проклятого смога.
Поздно.
Мы оба отравлены,

оба,
и поцелуй в этом смраде и тлене
как обоюдное отравленье ...
Рамки инструкций
на кленах и вязах
«Как целоваться в противогазах»
В барах повесили лозунг-находку:
«Можно спокойно дышать
лишь сквозь водку».
И только радио
на все кладет,
горланя радостно:
«А смог идет ...»
Кто там,
шатаясь, бредет по панели
с детским печальным лицом Паганеля?
Миллер?
Артур?
Он мне шепчет замедленно:
«Пахнет кострами,
охотой за ведьмами ...»
Кашляет Миллер,
худой,
остролицый.
Миллер в пророчестве страшном суров:
«Будут еще костры инквизиций.
Смог —
это дым от грядущих костров».
От смога неловко крылом заслоняясь,
жадный до тайн
и усталый от тайн,
на домике собственных книг,
словно аист,
тревожно стоит доброклювый Апдайк.
«Женя,
людей так жестоко надули,
землю поставив на ложных китах,
и надрывается
от натуги
все человечество,

будто кентавр.
И двуедино ржет и мычит оно
от двуединости делаясь злей.
Может быть, смог —
это бьющий мучительно
пар у кентавра из гневных ноздрей?»
Очки пытаясь протереть от смога,
у чьих-то книг, как у могильных плит,
с высокостью профессорского слога
мне Лоуэлл сквозь кашель говорит:
«Лишь у теней и книг — понятье чести.
Кого стыдиться? Лишь теней стыжусь.
И я продукт теней. Я — это вместе
Алеша Карамазов и Сен-Жюст.
Я верю в историческое мщенье,
в отмщенье неба за разврат, распад.
Быть может, смог — возвышенные тени,
которые за низость мира мстят?»
Ален Гинзберг —
лукавый пророк-павиан —
бьет в косматую грудь,
словно в бубен шаман:
«Темь надвигается,
темь!
Пахнет кромешным адом.
Нет оправданья тем,
кто может дышать этим смрадом!
В мире моральных пустот,
в мире тумана и хаоса
стоит чего-то лишь тот,
кто задыхается . . .
Все лжеидеи,
все лжеморали
небо,
чадя столько лет,
измарали.
Небо обратно шлет эту нудь —
не продохнуть!»
Но где-то над смогом,
над чадным вчера и сегодня

грохочет Уитмена бас,
будто рык Саваофа:
«Э-гей!
Задыхаться — нехитрое дело у пропасти.
А вы продышитесь,
а вы продышитесь!
Попробуйте!
Вздохните все вместе!
Увидите —
только вздохнете,
и смог, словно призрак,
дыханием с неба смахнете . . .»
И чудилось мне,
замерев, ожидала эпоха,
как сдвига вселенского,
нашего общего вздоха.

[*Знамя*, 1967]

INDEX OF TRANSLATORS

KUNITZ, STANLEY

MEZHAKOFF-KORIAKIN, IGOR (with Dutton)

REAVEY, GEORGE

INDEX OF FIRST LINES